TRAUMA-INFORMED PRACTICES FOR THE CLASSROOM AND BEYOND

LAURA B. WALLER
WILLIAM N. BENDER

For additional information on trauma, teachers are encouraged to utilize this book's companion website:
https://traumahelpnow.com

For information:

Corwin
A Sage Company
2455 Teller Road
Thousand Oaks, California 91320
(800) 233-9936
www.corwin.com

Sage Publications Ltd.
1 Oliver's Yard
55 City Road
London EC1Y 1SP
United Kingdom

Sage Publications India Pvt. Ltd.
Unit No 323-333, Third Floor, F-Block
International Trade Tower Nehru Place
New Delhi 110 019
India

Sage Publications Asia-Pacific Pte. Ltd.
18 Cross Street #10-10/11/12
China Square Central
Singapore 048423

Printed in the United States of America

Paperback ISBN 978-1-0719-3651-1

This book is printed on acid-free paper.

Vice President and Editorial Director:
 Monica Eckman
Publisher: Jessica Allan
Content Development Editor: Mia Rodriguez
Senior Editorial Assistant: Natalie Delpino
Production Editor: Vijayakumar
Copy Editor: Melinda Masson
Typesetter: TNQ Tech Pvt. Ltd.
Proofreader: Girish Sharma
Indexer: TNQ Tech Pvt. Ltd.
Cover Designer: Scott Van Atta
Marketing Manager: Olivia Bartlett

24 25 26 27 28 10 9 8 7 6 5 4 3 2 1

CONTENTS

This book has a companion website with additional information on trauma (**https://traumahelpnow.com**). Teachers are encouraged to utilize that additional information.

Note From the Publisher: The authors have provided video and web content throughout the book that is available to you through QR (quick response) codes. To read a QR code, you must have a smartphone or tablet with a camera. We recommend that you download a QR code reader app that is made specifically for your phone or tablet brand.

Videos may also be accessed at **https://traumahelpnow.com**

ABOUT THE AUTHORS

 **Laura B. Waller, MS/MA,** is a former elementary school teacher, an author, a National Certified Counselor, and a Licensed Professional Counselor. She holds a master's degree in elementary education from Johns Hopkins University and a second master's degree in clinical mental health counseling from Capella University. Waller is also an ADHD-Certified Clinical Services Provider. She entered the counseling field after a number of years as a teacher in elementary classrooms in North Carolina and Washington, DC. This classroom background yields a unique developmental perspective when Waller is working therapeutically with children, teens, and their families. She currently provides individual and family therapy for clients in the Northern Virginia (NOVA) area ranging in age from 8 to 60+. She also hosts monthly seminars and groups aimed at supporting parents with a particular focus on raising neurodivergent children. Waller has led numerous workshops for churches and schools in the NOVA area with a specific focus on communication between teens and parents as well as using emotional support animals in a therapeutic setting.

Waller is active in several professional associations, including the American Counseling Association (ACA) and Northern Virginia Licensed Professional Counselors (NVLPC). She has coauthored three books in education, most recently *RTI and Differentiated Reading in the K–8 Classroom* by Solution Tree Press (2011).

William N. Bender, PhD, has had a long and distinguished career in education, teaching in public school for several years and in higher education for some 26 years at Bluefield State College in West Virginia, Rutgers University in New Jersey, and the University of Georgia. He has written 36 books in special and general education. With his retirement, he has stepped back from his rigorous workshop schedule, which as recently as 2016 included some 40 workshop days per year. While the COVID-19 pandemic impacted his work, he has written four historical fiction novels and several educational books in recent years. He has delivered several professional development projects, including most recently a keynote for a virtual conference on project-based learning in Brazil in conjunction with his Corwin book *Project-Based Learning* (2012).

INTRODUCTION

Teachers, counselors, and clinicians are increasingly realizing the need for specific strategies to serve children and older students exposed to trauma, in any of its many forms. The COVID-19 outbreak resulted in virtually all students experiencing some degree of social isolation and/or absence of daily interaction with, and support from, their peer group. While it would be inaccurate to say that measures such as masking, at-home study, or social distancing resulted in significant trauma for all or even most students, research has shown that some students experienced those things as "devastating" traumatic events (Quirk, 2023; Sox & Min, 2023). In addition, the ever-growing immigrant population is impacting schools in every state, and many children are attending school with a lack of caregiver support in the home, thus bringing an even wider range of social isolation—and perhaps some trauma issues—to school for teachers and clinicians to address.

Research both prior to and after the recent pandemic has indicated that between 46% and 75% of children are exposed to trauma, with some portion of those students being exposed quite frequently (Morin, 2023). Further, research shows that trauma can lead to more involved, longer-term health or mental health problems (National Child Traumatic Stress Network, n.d.). In fact, in the most extreme cases, it is not an overstatement to say some students live in a persistent emotional crisis because of the ongoing trauma in their lives. These students experience life in an unpredictable environment in which any one or any combination of traumatic event(s) creates extremely adverse conditions, including inappropriate behaviors in school and at home and ultimately longer-term physical and mental health issues. These traumas may include food insecurity, parents with addiction, or constant movement from one foster placement to another, as well as the typical array of issues such as emotional, physical, or sexual abuse; neglect; mental illness; or incarceration of a parent.

Moreover, while any individual trauma can impact a student negatively over the long term (Morin, 2023), some students are exposed to repeated trauma. Pre-pandemic evidence indicates that almost two thirds of the 17,000 respondents reported exposure to at least one adverse childhood event (ACE) such as those listed earlier, and more than 20% reported experiencing three or more trauma events during childhood (Centers for Disease Control and Prevention, 2021). However, during the pandemic and post-pandemic period, that percentage increased to reveal that 73.1% of students are exposed to at least one ACE (Sox & Min, 2023).

Perhaps as many as 10%–16% of the school population is exposed to ACEs on a repeated or long-term basis. Such children may develop many mental health problems, up to and including post-traumatic stress disorder, or PTSD (Morin, 2023). Data indicate that as many as 15% of girls and 6% of boys who are exposed to trauma do develop PTSD, and as one might expect, the incidence is higher among students exposed to certain types of trauma, such as physical abuse or other violence in the home (U.S. Department of Veterans Affairs, 2022). The variety of negative symptoms that might be associated with PTSD in children is virtually unlimited, and teachers and clinicians must be prepared to deal with these issues.

In today's classroom and clinical practice spaces, professionals need highly specific, detailed information on strategies that can be implemented to assist students exposed to ACEs over time. This book aims directly at that need. While general ideas for creating a highly structured classroom, in order to assist students exposed to various ACEs, are certainly needed, this book is intended to be much more specific. Herein, specific instructional and clinical strategies are described such that any practicing professional—and, in many cases, parents of children exposed to trauma—can implement them.

The strategies discussed herein are aimed at students across the age span, and each is presented in sufficient detail so as to be implemented by a caring, involved professional. Some strategies are more appropriate for specific age groups. Some strategies can be implemented in a classroom setting while others are more suited for a clinical counseling environment. Some of the strategies herein can easily be implemented by a teacher who may be searching diligently for something to due to help a particular student, whereas other strategies may best be implemented at the individual school level. Still, in preparing professionals to work with students exposed to trauma, particularly repeated trauma, all these strategies should be considered. Both teachers and clinicians will need every possible tool available in order to offer the best services to students exposed to ACEs on a repeated basis. This book will include strategies for use with all students exposed to trauma, regardless of the duration or frequency of trauma exposure. Please note that we will use the terms *ACEs* and *trauma* interchangeably throughout this text.

Each of the authors has years of experience working with challenging children and teens, many of whom were exposed to trauma. While both authors are experienced public school teachers, Laura B. Waller, MS/MA, is now a practicing clinician working therapeutically with children, teens, and their families in her practice. She is an ADHD-Certified Clinical Services Provider and routinely implements many of the strategies included herein for students with an array of presenting problems, including students exposed to trauma.

Since his public school years teaching students with special needs, William N. Bender, PhD, has published a wide variety of books on disciplinary strategies for special needs classrooms and interventions for children and teens with extensive behavioral issues. Likewise, he has implemented many of the practices described herein with students exposed to trauma. The practical experience and expertise of these authors, coupled with the research cited for each strategy, provide professionals with some degree of confidence in the use of these techniques in their classroom and clinical practice.

We hope and believe that these strategies can be an important resource for teachers, counselors, and, in many instances, parents. With that in mind, we have chosen to develop a fairly extensive companion website (https://traumahelpnow.com) for this book to allow either individual study or a more involved professional in-service focused on this text. The website includes resource lists, additional websites, and/or video suggestions to provide more extensive information, tips for strategy intervention, and study guide questions. We hope this increases the usefulness of this book for you, and we encourage you to use those resources to enhance your services to these students who, so very much, need our help.

REFERENCES

Centers for Disease Control and Prevention. (2021, April 6). *About the CDC-Kaiser ACE study*. Retrieved from https://cdc.gov/violenceprevention/aces/about.html

Morin, A. (2023, November 20). *Understanding the effects of childhood trauma*. Verywell Mind. Retrieved from https://www.verywellmind.com/what-are-the-effects-of-childhood-trauma-4147640

National Child Traumatic Stress Network. (n.d.). *About child trauma*. Retrieved from https://www.nctsn.org/what-is-child-trauma/about-child-trauma#

Quirk, M. (2023, February 9). The benefits of mindfulness education in schools. *Psychology Today*. Retrieved from https://www.psychologytoday.com/us/blog/evidence-based-living/202302/the-benefits-of-mindfulness-education-in-schools

Sox, D. M., & Min, H. (2023, January 21). *Mentoring children with traumatic experiences*. Youth-Nex. Retrieved from https://youthnexblog.education. virginia.edu/?p=2391#

U.S. Department of Veterans Affairs. (2022, September 22). *How common is PTSD in children and teens?* Retrieved from https://www.ptsd.va.gov/ understand/common/common_children_teens.asp

CHAPTER 1

CHILDHOOD AND TEEN TRAUMA

KIDS LIVING IN CRISIS

Most teachers and counselors have experienced a child or adolescent whom they could never seem to reach, the one who was always mad, fighting, shouting, or, in the other extreme, shy to the point of being completely withdrawn from the world. Veteran professionals in either role can spot such deeply injured kids within 20 minutes of meeting them, based on their unusual behaviors or lack of engagement. While many causal factors contribute to these types of unusual behavioral patterns, such behaviors, in some cases, may indicate that the child or adolescent has been exposed to trauma.

Kids exposed to trauma, particularly repeated trauma, usually seem to the practiced professional to be highly reactive to anything in their environment, and perhaps more extreme in their behaviors. While many children experience trauma on occasion, some children and teenagers experience extreme trauma repeatedly. Some children and adolescents live in persistently stressful environments due to repeated trauma. This type of unpredictable and frequent trauma can lead to anxiety, depression, or a litany of other mental health issues among children or teens (Morin, 2023). In fact, data show that some children and teens exposed to adverse childhood experiences (ACEs) repeatedly present with actual post-traumatic stress disorder, or PTSD (U.S. Department of Veterans Affairs, 2022). Further, home environments that are characterized by parental addiction, poverty, physical abuse or neglect, or other extreme trauma often lead to highly inappropriate behaviors at school or elsewhere.

Of course, not all trauma leads to negative outcomes. A child who was socially isolated during the COVID-19 pandemic, from 2020 through perhaps 2021, probably experienced some degree of trauma associated with that social isolation (Conklin, 2023), but in most cases this does not lead to life-changing, long-term problems. Further, many other life events may cause some trauma in a child's life, such as parental divorce, death of a parent or sibling, or simply a family move from one locale to another. Again, in the majority of these instances, the change may be a traumatic event, but the impact of the trauma is not long-term, and not nearly as debilitating as the extreme, repeated trauma mentioned previously. Further, the duration of the trauma impacts the outcomes; abuse or neglect that takes place for months or years will impact a child much more so than neglect that is observed and addressed in a shorter time frame (Morin, 2023; Quirk, 2023).

EXAMPLES OF POTENTIAL TRAUMA

Vignette 1.1 Samantha: Possible neglect

Samantha was a freshman student who had repeated absences across multiple years of school beginning in seventh grade. Her grades consistently fell below a C average. Throughout her freshman year, Samantha was required to take remedial classes in core subjects, specifically language arts classes. These remedial classes failed to prove successful due to increased levels of truancy. When Samantha was in attendance, teachers noted a lack of involvement and increased sleeping during class. The school reported multiple attempts to involve her parents in the concern for her failing grades and lack of school attendance. Despite the school's efforts, Samantha's parents were consistently unavailable for phone calls or meetings requested by administration and guidance counselors. The parents' continued lack of involvement or concern alerted the counselors to the possibility of neglect.

Vignette 1.2 Diego: Withdrawal and possible neglect

Diego was an adolescent who rarely seemed to interact with anyone at school or on the bus. Most frequently, he would simply mumble a one-syllable answer to any question the teacher asked, and he always seemed to be withdrawn whenever anyone tried to engage him in conversation. He never looked anyone in the eye, and often turned away when someone spoke to him. He seemed to have no friends, and to trust no one. His self-imposed aloneness was so obvious that two of his teachers in middle school visited the counselor with their concerns.

Vignette 1.3 Tamara: Possible physical abuse

Tamara was often the loudest student in the group when on the playground or in the hallway. However, in class, her friendly personality seemed to transform, as if she was terrified in the class environment. If she made a mistake and the teacher corrected her, she seemed to completely shut down emotionally. Sometimes when corrected on her classwork, she would say that she was going to "tell her mama" that the teacher was picking on her, or that the teacher wasn't being fair. The teacher began to feel that Tamara might be overly dependent on her mother for some reason, so the teacher asked the counselor to have a talk with Tamara and her mom.

It was later discovered that the mother was very protective of her daughter for a very good reason. The father, who was then no longer in the home, had been physically abusive to both Tamara and her mother. Thus, the overprotective mother was easily explained.

In situations like this, overprotectiveness can, in and of itself, become an issue, because students are not allowed to discover how to deal with the challenges of school and/or their social life without parental intervention. Students like Tamara may try to get their overprotective parent involved at even higher grade levels whenever homework is not done or the student fails an exam. Parents who are overprotective may be personally overwhelmed with guilt about their earlier failure to protect their child, and they may try to fight every battle for their child. This alone can limit a child's independence and growth.

These are merely several composite examples of how ongoing trauma may impact children and adolescents, and these examples represent problems that are not all that uncommon. However, all professionals should tread lightly when they begin to suspect that a child may be exposed to trauma at home. Repeated trauma certainly represents one potential reason for inappropriate behavior, or extreme shyness, but there are many reasons for childhood and adolescent misbehaviors other than trauma. In fact, almost all children misbehave some, and only a percentage of kids—maybe 15% to 20%—are truly challenged by repeated long-term trauma (Morin, 2023). However, if we teachers and counselors see only the behavior problems and concern ourselves only with the classroom disruptions that problem behavior brings, we might miss seeing the fundamental cause—the trauma in the background of some of the students in our charge. Personally, we authors have realized that we are much more in touch with our students' and clients' needs when we question why a child might present an array of concerning behaviors. Sometimes, then, we can more readily spot the traumas or other challenges that students might face, and we can begin to make discrete inquiries about them, as needed.

COMPLEXITY OF TRAUMA

Unfortunately, trauma experienced by some children is often more complex than merely one ACE or life circumstance. The complexities of trauma to which a child is exposed may involve interactions between current trauma and the trauma the child's parents experienced in their early life. The term intergenerational trauma has recently been used to describe this phenomenon (Rosenthal, 2021). Such complex trauma may involve more than one type of trauma over one or more generations (poverty, food insecurity, abuse, or addiction).

First, it should also be obvious that if parents of a student were, themselves, raised in a dysfunctional home environment—unpredictable and persistently stressful—then it is quite likely that they will raise their children in a similar environment. In this situation, interventions for the trauma experienced by the child today may require some rather involved family counseling to look for, and ultimately alleviate, this type of complex trauma interaction. Clinicians often see situations in which trauma experienced by children is to be expected, based on their home environment, and in many cases, such trauma may be based on trauma that was experienced by one or more of their parents during their childhood.

It is the professionals' role, then—teacher and counselor working together—to tease out the reasons some children behave as they do, and to develop effective strategies for reaching and teaching those students. While all children misbehave from time to time, identifying situations in which such inappropriate behavior stems from trauma in the child's life is critical, in order to have any real chance of success in serving them. This teasing-out process typically begins with some questions:

▸ Is there poverty in the home? Does that lead to hunger?
▸ Does this student get a meal at home each day?
▸ Does this student receive regular medical and dental care?
▸ Is there physical or mental abuse in this child's family?
▸ Does this child seem depressed or withdrawn? Do I ever see them talking to friends?
▸ Does this child have brothers or sisters with similar problematic behaviors?

► Does this child appear deeply, emotionally injured somehow?

► Does this student display emotions or behaviors that seem unnormal or extreme?

► Is this child overly shy or withdrawn?

► Is there a tendency to overuse or pay extensive attention to social media by this child?

While these questions can give teachers and counselors a starting point, none can really focus us enough to point directly to the answers we need. For example, knowing the poverty rate and the percentages of children experiencing abuse doesn't really summarize the reality for specific students or clients, and statistics don't really represent the actual experience; a statistic on hunger or poverty is not the same as a gnawing hunger in one's gut. Further, any and all of the life-changing challenges mentioned thus far can create deep, abiding emotional scars for some students but not for others, and those scars will result in different behaviors in different kids.

Also, the various "causal factors" that might, in some cases, lead to trauma often overlap, and any of these threats to development can interact with and influence other negative factors in a child's life. Finally, none of the questions listed earlier really tease out the specifics on how many kids are raised by severely traumatized adults. Of course, it is frequently the case that a parent's life disruptions do negatively impact their kids' lives. Divorce, parental addictions, moves that involve attending a new school district, and other life changes impact children and teens in many ways. However, it is also possible that such life events do not lead to trauma. Further, some traumatized parents raise reasonably normal kids, particularly if there is a mitigating influence toward normalcy in the child's life. A next-door neighbor, a minister, a rabbi, an older sibling, or a coach might serve as a stable role model or a strength for a child in a home characterized by trauma. This could, and quite often does, mitigate the effects of the trauma for some students. Several of the strategies described later in this book are focused on providing this type of significant other adult in the child's life, in order to help alleviate the negative impact of traumatic circumstances.

GETTING A HANDLE ON TRAUMA RISK FACTORS

To get a handle on trauma, we suggest that teachers and counselors begin by asking the right questions. All too often, when presented with a misbehavior or even consistent misbehavior from a child, we might ask (generally to ourselves) something like "What's going on with this kid?" or some other version of "What's wrong with you?" However, we and most other veteran teachers and counselors have learned that we can get a better handle on these students if we transform those questions into something like "What has happened to you?" or "What life circumstances led to this behavior?" Using those questions, we can get a much richer picture of deeply injured children (Adams, 2013), and moreover, those latter questions often lead directly to specific intervention strategies for various types of traumas at various ages.

From that perspective, then, teachers and counselors should begin with a solid understanding of the many risk factors that can, and frequently do, lead to trauma among students. The litany of risk factors associated with childhood injury is seemingly endless, and while not all of these can be described herein, a brief discussion of some of the most impactful risk factors is warranted. As noted, these risk factors often co-present or overlap in some ways, and while that brings increased complexity to an individual student's situation, professionals must begin somewhere, and this is the best point we have. At a minimum, factors such as poverty, hunger, parental addiction, child abuse, depression, and suicidal thoughts must be considered when dealing with children and teens exposed to trauma (Morin, 2023; National Institute on Drug Abuse [NIDA], n.d.; Rind, Tromovitch, & Bauserman, 1998; Whealin & Barnett, 2007). Other factors such as social media usage may likewise impact children in traumatic fashion, though much less is known about what role these factors play in trauma.

Poverty

Data on poverty over the last few decades have been fairly consistent. Creamer, Shrider, Burns, and Chen (2022) used census data compiled in 2021 and documented a poverty rate of 11.6% of the U.S. population, suggesting that 37.9 million people live in poverty. They noted that this was very similar to the 2020 poverty rate. While the poverty level does fluctuate from time to time, there has been a slight downward trend in overall poverty over recent decades. For example, Creamer et al. noted a decrease in childhood poverty in the 2021 data. However, racial disparities were quite apparent in those data. Only 2.8% of white children lived in poverty, whereas 8.1% of Black children and 8.4% of Hispanic children experienced poverty in the home (Creamer et al., 2022). While various minority groups may be delineated using a variety of terms, we have chosen for this book to utilize the terms chosen by the original authors and/or government sources in the various studies, which is why this book contains various terms such as *Black* or *African American*, *Hispanic* or *Latino*, and *Native American* or *Indigenous* to refer to the same groups in different chapters.

In addition to those living below the poverty line, nearly 33% of people in the United States live in households that are only slightly above the poverty line. Also, poverty rates differ from state to state, with the highest poverty in Kentucky, Alabama, New Mexico, Mississippi, and Louisiana, with the poverty rate ranging between 19% and 22% in those states. The data also show that poverty rates are persistently higher in rural and inner-city areas than in other areas of the country. Finally, many experts use the term *extreme poverty* to indicate those living on $2 per day, excluding government benefits. Recent data show that 1.5 million U.S. households, which include some 2.8 million children, live in extreme poverty. As one might imagine, these extremely impoverished homes are most closely associated with kids exposed to trauma, but the effort to identify the root cause of the trauma is much more complex, as poverty frequently overlaps with other factors such as food insecurity, single-parent households, and/or drug addiction in the home.

Childhood Hunger

The term *food insecurity* is used to designate homes where meals are sometimes not provided. Households with "low food security" are homes where availability of food at mealtime was not assured at least once within the previous 12 months. Moreover, homes with "very low food security" are homes in which receiving any food at all was not a certainty. In 2022, rising food costs contributed to 28% of U.S. households going hungry at some point (Annie E. Casey Foundation, 2023). Moreover, during 2022 in 11 states, approximately 32% of children were not eating, at least occasionally, because of the price of food. Again, different ethnic groups experienced this differently. For example, 21% of white children experienced some hunger, whereas 38% of Black children and 37% of Latino and multiracial children experienced hunger, which was associated with rising food costs. The parallel between these figures, when aggregated by ethnicity, and the poverty figures provided earlier is nothing less than striking. Clearly, poverty and food insecurity often go hand in hand, and both impact children in certain minority groups much more so than other children.

Data further reveal that families headed by single mothers experienced food insecurity in 24% of cases; this is much higher than in two-parent families. Also, while hunger can impact any family anywhere, more food insecurity was found in rural areas (Annie E. Casey Foundation, 2023). As one concrete example, Dr. Bender was recently teaching a Bible class in a drug rehabilitation center and worked with a 34-year-old white man we'll call Amos, who was recovering from a long-term addiction. His story exemplifies these complex causes of early childhood trauma.

Vignette 1.4 Amos's hunger and multiple ACEs

I was really young when Dad got addicted, and he didn't work for quite a while. Our power was cut off, and most of the time we didn't have much to eat. By then, Mom was gone, and Daddy and I were living out in the country in a trailer. One time, I was really hungry, but when I told Daddy, he just stayed in the bed and shouted at me to 'go get something out of the kitchen!' I must have been about 6 or 7 at the time, but I was old enough to know there wasn't anything to eat in the kitchen. Then I remembered that one of our neighbors raised free-range chickens, so I went over to their backyard and caught one. I just stole it. I remember breaking its neck, and building a fire in an old bucket out in the woods. I had to sneak back into Daddy's trailer to get the matches, and I had to pluck that chicken too. I'd seen my dad pluck feathers from doves he'd shot, so I knew how to do that. I didn't really clean that chicken because I didn't know how, but I got the feathers off, mostly off anyway, and then I just put it on top of the fire in the bucket. When the side of a leg got done, I just bit right into it. I had to eat something, and nobody ever figured out that I'd taken that chicken.

The intermingled trauma—food insecurity, poverty, and parental addiction—in Amos's life was devastating, and as an adult, he has been an addict himself, in and out of jail and several rehab programs. Several years ago, he had gotten clean and remained sober for four years while employed locally. He was then arrested again for drug use. Many trauma victims become addicts in their teen years, as did Amos, and then go through several intervention programs. Hopefully, one program or another will take hold, but any period of sobriety is a victory. Still, Amos's life is a telling example of the damage caused by exposure to multiple ACEs in childhood.

Amos still calls Dr. Bender periodically, and as of the writing of this book, he has completed eight successful months in another drug rehab setting. Again, each of those months represents a singular, and very important, victory for Amos. We wish him well.

Anxiety and Depression

Anxiety and depression are separate disorders but often go hand in hand. While everyone feels anxious from time to time, a pervasive, long-term, and nonspecific anxiousness is more serious than simple fears or worries about various situations in life. Such pervasive, nonspecific anxiety can be quite pervasive and debilitating. Social anxiety, phobias, and other types of longer-term anxiety can, in and of themselves, negatively impact one's life, and such pervasive anxiousness often leads to depression. Because these disorders often coexist, and because the treatments for each are similar, they are often described together. Further, these two, anxiety and depression, are some of the most common results of exposure to multiple ACEs over time.

Depression is sometimes experienced based on circumstances without anxiousness (death of a parent, loss of a boyfriend/girlfriend, etc.), and again, those brief depressions are common to everyone. In contrast, clinical depression (sometimes called major depression) is defined as a mental disorder characterized by at least two weeks of persistent low mood that seems to be independent of situations or setting. Data collected during the COVID-19 pandemic of 2020–2021 indicated that both anxiety and depression among children were increasing (Reinberg, 2021; Scott, Marcu, Anderson, Newman, & Schoenebeck, 2023), and this will make these issues more pressing for both teachers and clinicians.

Clinical depression is more common in children after puberty and is frequently related to social anxieties that arise during the preteen and teen years. However, children as young as three have been diagnosed with clinical depression (National Institutes of Health, 2018). In some extreme cases, clinical depression may lead to suicide attempts (Anxiety and Depression Association of America [ADAA], 2021), but again, this is more likely in older individuals than in very young children. Because depression is more common as children mature into adolescents, the relationship between depression and suicide becomes more critical as children grow older. Still, not all children who contemplate or attempt suicide are clinically depressed, and not all depression leads to suicide attempts.

Children whose parents manifest clinical depression are at a greater risk of being depressed themselves (ADAA, 2021). Further, depression affects all ages, races, and social groups. Depression impacts both genders, but research has shown that girls are more likely to develop depression during adolescence than are boys (ADAA, 2021). Finally, between 2% and 3% of children ages 6 to 12, and 6% to 8% of teens, may have clinical depression.

Suicide

Suicide and attempted suicide in many cases result from ongoing trauma in a child's or teen's life, and this problem seems to be growing. Suicide is the second-leading cause of death among teens between 14 and 18 today (Ivey-Stephenson et al.,

2023). The Centers for Disease Control and Prevention (CDC, 2023) reported that 49,500 persons in the United States took their own lives in 2022 and four-fifths of those were men, making that the highest number of suicides in one year, ever (Newsmax, 2023). While this may be associated with the COVID-19 pandemic, it is too early to state that for certain. Further, the suicide rate across the age range has been steadily increasing since 2000, with notable dips in the total number of suicides in 2019 and again in 2020 (ABC15 Arizona, 2018; Newsmax, 2023). The lower number of suicides at the height of the COVID-19 outbreak seems consistent with data from other crisis periods in recent history. For example, the suicide rate frequently remains stable or goes down as wars break out, because in such crisis periods families, communities, and the entire country seem to "pull together" and support each other more.

Still, the year-to-year trend documents increased suicides over the last 25 years. Many factors have been mentioned for this including increased rates of depression, limited mental health services, and increased social media usage, coupled with social isolation and the availability of guns. Suicide attempts involving guns succeed much more frequently than suicide attempts using other methods, making the increasing number of homeowners owning firearms a growing concern.

Fortunately, as noted earlier, not all depression leads to suicide, and not all children and teens who consider suicide actually attempt it. *Suicide ideation* is a term used for the contemplation of suicide, in the absence of an actual suicide attempt. In 2019, data show that 18.8% of teens considered suicide at one point; some 24.1% of females and 13.3% of males in that study considered suicide (Ivey-Stephenson et al., 2023). Suicide ideation may or may not involve making a plan for how to undertake suicide (e.g., "I know where my mother keeps her sleeping pills, and I'll take the whole jar!"), but in suicide ideation cases, no actions relative to that plan are attempted.

In contrast to suicide ideation, a suicide attempt involves actual actions taken with the express purpose of doing oneself bodily harm or ending one's life. The data also show that 11% of females and 6.6% of males report attempted suicide (Ivey-Stephenson et al., 2023). When children and teens do attempt suicide, they are often not successful, though the method they may use does impact the number of successful suicides. Again, when guns are involved, the likelihood of success is much higher than using other methods such as taking pills or attempting to hang oneself. Because guns are more frequently used by males in suicide attempts, males are more likely to succeed in ending their own life than are females.

Suicide, suicide attempts, and suicide ideation also vary by age and sex. According to the CDC (2023), no suicide deaths were reported over a six-year period from 2008 through 2014 for children under the age of five, though suicides were reported in older age groups. Suicide rates typically peak between adolescence and the early to mid-30s. Once again, the most recent data continue to indicate that boys are more likely to commit suicide successfully than are girls, though females manifest more suicide ideation than do boys. The CDC reports that the suicide rate among males in 2021 was four times higher than among females, and while males make up 50% of the population, they account for nearly 80% of suicides. Again, this is probably related to the fact that males choose to use firearms much more frequently than do females for suicide attempts, and those suicide attempts are much more likely to succeed.

With the recent increase in news coverage of sexual identity issues over the last decade or so, researchers have begun to include sexual preferences and sexual orientation in their research designs as they study suicide. Ivey-Stephenson et al. (2023) indicate that 23% of school-aged lesbians reported a suicide attempt within the last year, compared with 16% of students who indicated they were "not sure" about their sexuality. Only 6% of heterosexual students reported a suicide attempt. These results suggest that professionals may need to pay increased attention to individuals with sexual identity questions or nontraditional sexual identities.

With these data in mind, teachers and clinicians, like all mental health professionals, have an obligation to be cognizant of the indicators that a child might be suffering from long-term clinical depression, which may lead to suicide attempts. Box 1.1 presents a list of indicators of both depression and suicide. If any of these indicators is observed, the teacher should certainly write a brief, dated note, describing what they saw that was of concern, and then bring that information to the attention of a counselor or school principal. Jointly, those professionals can then determine an appropriate course of action.

Box 1.1 Indicators of depression and suicide

- Family history of depression or suicide
- Changes in social media use
- Impulsivity
- Increased recklessness or risky behaviors
- Feelings of helplessness
- Unusual interest in dying
- Bullying or consistently a bully victim
- Withdrawal from friends or family

- Frequent or pervasive sadness
- Changes in eating or sleeping habits
- Decline in quality of schoolwork
- Voicing feelings of loss or rejection
- Giving away personal items
- Aggressive or disruptive behaviors
- Heavy social media use
- Exposure to or threats of violence
- Physical symptoms related to extreme stress such as explosive emotions, stomachaches, headaches, and fatigue

Social Media Usage and Trauma

Child and teenage usage of social media platforms has increased drastically over the last 10–15 years, and many psychologists and counselors believe this may have led to increased mental health problems among the youth of today (Conklin, 2023; Scott et al., 2023). By 2022, approximately 200 school districts filed a federal lawsuit against a number of social media technology companies for creating addictive social media platforms and causing a mental health crisis among adolescents. Also, similar lawsuits have been filed against social media companies by various states. The companies include Meta (owner of Facebook and Instagram), ByteDance (owner of TikTok), Snap Inc. (owner of Snapchat), and Google (owner of YouTube; Conklin, 2023). On these platforms, according to the plaintiffs in many of these lawsuits, students are increasingly exposed to potential bullying; to dangerous content, such as sexual or violent content; and sometimes to adult predators. The lawsuits further claim that the addictive nature of these social media platforms has led to increased anxiety, depression, and suicide ideation among youth today.

In March 2023, the Surgeon General of the United States, Dr. Vivek Murthy, issued a warning about the growing mental health crisis, which may be caused by increased social media usage (Conklin, 2023). It is also possible that the homeschooling resulting from the COVID-19 pandemic tended to isolate children and teens at home, and with many more children doing schoolwork online, these kids were exposed to increased screen time without the moderating influence of a teacher. Clearly, unchecked and unmonitored social media usage is becoming a very real concern.

Of course, these lawsuits represent a relatively new issue, and while there is limited research linking social media use with childhood trauma (Scott et al., 2023), this linkage has not yet been fully researched. With these questions unanswered, we decided to merely present herein the suggestion that trauma may be either caused or exacerbated by extensive social media usage. Clearly, both teachers and parents should carefully monitor the screen time and social media usage of children and teens, as well as ask questions about postings on these platforms that might make children feel uncomfortable. Social media usage may represent more of a danger to children and teens than originally believed.

Abuse and Neglect

Child abuse and neglect are pervasive problems and impact one in seven children, though the CDC (2022) suggests that this is probably a low estimate because many cases go unreported. The CDC specifies several types of abuse, any of which can traumatize a child or adolescent. Further, any of these can lead to either clinical depression or suicide attempts, so all of these represent significant concerns.

1. **Physical abuse:** the intentional use of physical force that can result in physical injury. This includes hitting, kicking, shaking, burning, or other use of force against someone under the age of 18.
2. **Emotional abuse:** parental or caregiver behaviors that harm a child's sense of self-worth or emotional well-being. This includes name-calling, shaming, rejecting, withdrawing or withholding love, and threatening children.
3. **Neglect:** a failure on the part of the parent or caregiver to meet a child's basic needs such as housing, food, clothing, education, and access to medical or dental care, or simply failure to have the child's feelings validated and appropriately responded to. Ignoring a child's feelings is a form of neglect.

(CDC, 2022)

Given these definitions, more than 600,000 children are abused each year in the United States, and those data from 2021 probably are an underestimate.

Specifically, the COVID-19 pandemic was restricting school attendance that year, and limited attendance in school may have prevented professionals from noticing some cases of child abuse (National Children's Alliance, 2023).

We do know that young children are somewhat more likely to be abused than older children, with 28% of all child abuse cases involving children two years old or younger (National Children's Alliance, 2023). Among the reported cases of abuse, 76% of the children suffer from neglect without any physical abuse. Further, 16% of children are physically abused, with 10% of these children being sexually abused and 0.2% being victims of sex trafficking.

Both sex and race impact the frequency of child abuse and neglect (U.S. Administration for Children and Families, 2023). Girls are slightly more likely to be abused than boys (8.7 girls vs. 7.5 boys per 1,000). Also, Native American and Native Alaskan children are the children most likely to be abused (15.2 per 1,000), while African American children have the second-highest rate of abuse (13.1 per 1,000). As this breakdown indicates, rates of child abuse and neglect seem to roughly parallel socioeconomic factors for the various ethnic and racial groups, and thus poverty seems to be an important factor. Finally, to reiterate the seriousness of this issue, we note that 1,820 children died from abuse and neglect in 2021 (U.S. Administration for Children and Families, 2023).

Beyond poverty and food insecurity, other causes of abuse and neglect are complex. Data indicate that in the majority of cases—some 76%—the perpetrators of child abuse are parents. Each class of "other perpetrators" (including significant others of a single parent, other relatives, and non–family members) accounts for less than 9% of abuse cases, respectively (National Children's Alliance, 2023). With the majority of child and teen abuse cases involving only neglect, it can be quite difficult for teachers and clinicians to identify situations where abuse occurs. Where there are physical bruises from physical abuse in the home, the abuse is more observable to professionals at school than merely neglect, and thus neglect is more often overlooked. Nevertheless, professionals should note obvious things such as children who seemingly never have new or clean clothes, or children who appear at school unwashed or otherwise unkept. These may indicate child neglect.

Again, professionals must always approach such situations with extreme caution since each of the various indicators of physical abuse or neglect can also simply result from the types of things all children do. Children and teens do get dirty on the school bus, tear their clothes, or have accidents that result in bruises, broken bones, lacerations, and even burns, and these do not necessarily indicate abuse. Repeated examples of these, of course, would certainly indicate that some questions should be asked. Fortunately, in recent years, with increased awareness of the child abuse problem, all professionals are more prepared to approach a potential problem, and almost all school districts have procedures whereby teachers should document their observations and concerns to others at the school.

Sexual Abuse of Children and Teens

The CDC (2022) defines sexual abuse as pressuring or forcing a child to engage in sexual acts, which may include fondling, penetration, or exposing a child to other sexual activities. Some data indicate that child sexual abuse may be the most common type of physical abuse of children. Overall, these data indicate the following:

- One in five girls and one in twenty boys are victims of child sexual abuse each year.
- Self-report studies indicate higher rates of abuse than the documented cases that show up in legal proceedings. These self-report data suggest that 20% of females and 10% of males recall a childhood sexual assault/ abuse incident.
- During one year, approximately 16% of all youth, ages 14 and 17, were sexually victimized.
- Children living with only one parent were more likely to be sexually victimized.

(Rind et al., 1998; Whealin & Barnett, 2007).

However, there is some good news among this relatively bleak picture of childhood victimization. Overall sexual victimization of children and teens has declined in recent decades as our society has focused more on this problem. Still, many children are victimized, and the overall impact of sexual victimization on children can be devastating, making this one type of ACE that is likely to have long-term, and very negative, consequences. A child victim of prolonged sexual assault will typically develop low self-esteem, feelings of worthlessness, and an abnormal view of social or sexual relationships. These children frequently seem to withdraw, have few close friends, and have very limited social interaction at school or elsewhere (National Center for Victims of Crime, 2023). Further, extreme anxiety disorders, eating disorders, PTSD, major depression, and even suicide attempts are common among victims of sexual abuse. With these potentially devastating consequences resulting from this specific type of trauma, all professionals must be vigilant in looking for indicators of this problem, and some of the main indicators are presented in Box 1.2.

Box 1.2 Indicators of childhood sexual abuse

- Persistent and inappropriate sexual play with peers, toys, animals, or themselves
- A girl inserting objects in her vagina or sexually aggressive behavior with others
- Detailed and overly sophisticated understanding of sexual behavior
- Sexual themes in the child's artwork, stories, or play
- Fear of going home, or expressing a desire to live in a foster home or institution
- Regressive behavior (e.g., excessive clinginess or the sudden onset of behavior problems)
- Soiling and wetting the bed, when these were not formerly a problem
- Appearing disconnected or focused on fantasy worlds
- Sleep disturbances and nightmares
- Marked changes in appetite
- Fear states (e.g., anxiety, depression, phobias, obsession)
- Overly compliant behavior
- Extensive grooming behaviors
- Delinquent or aggressive behavior
- Increased inability to concentrate in school and/or sudden deterioration in school performance
- Truancy/running away from home
- Excessive seductive behavior and/or sexual activity
- Drug/alcohol abuse
- Prostitution or casual sexual encounters
- Self-mutilation (i.e., cutting of arms, legs; burning; homemade tattoos)
- Suicidal feelings and suicide attempts
- Fear of adults of the same sex as the abuser
- Siblings behaving like boyfriend and girlfriend or embarrassed when seen together

While all professionals must be aware of the indicators of sexual abuse, neither statistics nor indicators of a problem show the horrid emotional damage experienced by those who go through this type of trauma. Here is a real example of how sexual abuse, an addiction in the home, and food insecurity combined to create a complex interaction of ACEs—a persistent crisis—for two young girls.

Vignette 1.5 Tina and her sister: Partners in trauma

Tina (not her real name) was a very bright child being raised, along with her younger sister, by a single mom addicted to drugs in an urban area in South Carolina. She recalls her middle school and early high school years as ones of devastating poverty, hunger, and other trauma. She had to "steal Mama's pills and sell them at school" in order to get money to buy food for herself and for her younger sister. Moreover, both of those young girls had been victims of extended sexual abuse by a distant family member over a period of years. That person was ultimately convicted and put into prison, but the situation at home did not change as a result of that, at least in terms of food insecurity. The two young girls essentially had to raise themselves, and this complex interaction of multiple ACEs was devastating.

Tina and her sister, however, were a strength for each other, and while both, as young adults, have long-lasting emotional scars, both graduated high school and began college programs, essentially by pushing and challenging each other at every step. Some years later, Tina worked with the second author of this book, as a young adult, in a successful effort to improve her life and her education. She was successful by every standard, as was her sister. Tina's sister completed an associate's degree, and Tina completed several years of college. Both are now working, and are in stable long-term relationships.

While Tina had some earlier "control issues" (her term) that led to two failed marriages, she is now doing very well as a businessperson and raising her children. The resilience shown by Tina and her sister stemmed from the support they had from that close relationship to each other. They worked together to survive an array of ACEs, and ultimately leave a dysfunctional home and dysfunctional life behind. Both of these young women beat the odds.

Addiction in the Home

Research shows that 25% of children in the United States grow up in households where substance abuse is present, and children who grow up in such households are more than twice as likely to develop addictions themselves (American Addiction Centers, 2022; NIDA, n.d.). Further, such children demonstrate an array of behavioral and social problems including poor academic performance, conduct disorders in school, emotional or social disorders, lower self-esteem, increased anxiety or depression, and increased manifestations of risky behaviors such as early sexual encounters or early and frequent experimentation with illegal substances.

Substance abuse by parents also impacts children and adolescents in more subtle ways, making this issue harder for professionals to identify. The children impacted by these traumas tend to grow up to be untrusting of others, and may lack the ability to form solid, positive relationships. Timmen and Cermack (1985) described a condition that they refer to as "psychic numbing," a sense of estrangement or being detached to the point of feeling there is no place or group to which one truly belongs. These children are often quite limited in their ability to express intimacy, tenderness, or even sexual intimacy, and this detachment may lead to social isolation, difficulty in having intimate relationships, depression, or suicide at any point in life.

Further, it is not uncommon in households where parental addiction is present for children from very young ages to essentially raise themselves, as was the case in Vignette 1.5. In that instance, a 12-year-old girl began to steal and sell medications to help feed herself and her younger sibling. Further, children may even take on a caregiving role toward their own parents (e.g., feeding an addicted parent, helping a drunk mother clean herself), which is a complete reversal of the traditional caregiving role. Finally, and perhaps most damaging over the long term, is that children of addicted parents frequently begin to believe that the parental addiction is somehow their own fault (American Addiction Centers, 2022). They may feel that, had they done better in school or tried harder to help at home, the addicted parent may not have ever become addicted. These feelings, when they do develop, are quite traumatic, are damaging to the child's self-esteem, and can last well into adulthood. Box 1.3 presents some additional indicators that teachers and clinicians might observe in students being raised by addicted parents.

Box 1.3 Indicators of children with addicted parents

- Fear/mistrust of authority figures
- Inability to form close friendships
- Difficulty having fun
- Impulsivity
- Judging oneself harshly all the time
- Feelings of alienation, "different" from others
- Chronic anxiety
- Compulsive lying
- Secretive nature
- Lack of self-respect
- Manifestation of physical symptoms such as explosive emotions, stomachaches, headaches, and fatigue

---

QUANTIFYING TRAUMA: THE ACES STUDY

The ACEs described throughout this chapter represent only the most severe types of factors that may foster trauma in a child's life, and complex overlap or interactions among these can make any attempt to understand causal factors quite difficult. Perhaps the best way for teachers and clinicians to clarify these complex issues involves how many ACEs a child is exposed to prior to the age of 18. Felitti and colleagues (1998; see also Felitti & Anda, 2009) used a data set developed in a long-term study by the CDC (2021), working with Kaiser Permanente, to help understand these multiple risk factors. This was a very large study, conducted over a period of multiple years, and as such it has become one cornerstone of virtually all discussions of childhood and teen trauma today. While almost any type of lifetime event can cause trauma, the most common ACEs were listed by the CDC (2021) and others (Felitti & Anda, 2009; Felitti et al., 1998; Sporleder & Forbes, 2016). These are presented in Box 1.4.

Box 1.4 Original top 10 list of ACEs

- **Physical abuse:** any nonaccidental physical injury to the child, including striking, kicking, burning, or biting the child, or any action that results in a physical impairment or harms the child's health and welfare.
- **Emotional abuse:** emotional or psychological injury to the child as evidenced by a substantial change in behavior, emotional response or anxiety, depression, withdrawal, or aggressive behavior.

(Continued)

(Continued)

- **Physical neglect:** the failure of a parent or caregiver to provide food, clothing, shelter, education, medical care, or supervision such that the child's health, safety, and well-being are threatened with harm.
- **Emotional neglect:** the failure of a parent to provide needed emotional attention, support, recognition, love, and empathetic response such that the child's emotional health and development are threatened with harm.
- **Sexual abuse:** any act of sexual nature that uses the child for sexual gratification, including rape, molestation, prostitution, pornography, or other forms of sexual exploitation of children.
- **Loss of a parent:** discontinuation of contact with a parent by death, divorce, or abandonment.
- **Mother treated violently or other family violence:** being a witness to violence creates significant emotional and psychological damage due to the high stress experienced by the child.
- **Incarceration of a family member:** having any family member in jail can create substantial emotional issues, such as grief and loss, stigmatization, anxiety, and depression.
- **Having a mentally ill, depressed, or suicidal family member:** growing up in a family dealing with mental health issues can cause confusion, fear, anxiety, stress, and lack of attention and concern regarding the child's own emotional health.
- **Living with a drug-addicted or alcoholic family member:** drug and alcohol addiction of parents can negatively impact a child's sense of safety, predictability, stability, normalcy, connectedness, and attachment.

The first finding was nothing less than staggering: Nearly 50% of adults in this extensive study reported exposure to at least one type of ACE prior to the age of 18 (Felitti et al., 1998). Further, 25% had experienced two or more ACEs (CDC, 2021; Felitti & Anda, 2009; Felitti et al., 1998). Also, the data in the ACEs study documented a "graded-dose effect" between exposure to multiple ACEs and negative health and well-being outcomes later in life (CDC, 2021; Felitti & Anda, 2009). Adults who had experienced four or more ACEs prior to the age of 18 showed a fourfold increased risk for alcoholism, drug use, depression, smoking, and exposure to sexually transmitted disease, as well as increased suicide attempts. Simply put, the more ACEs a child or teen is exposed to, the more likely they are to be long-term negative outcomes ranging from heath issues to increased interactions with policing agencies and increased risky behaviors overall (CDC, 2021; Felitti et al., 1998).

As one rough indicator, exposure to six or more of the ACEs listed in Box 1.4 by the age of 18 seems to be even more indicative of negative long-term outcomes.

The good news herein is that while many persons experience some trauma as children or in their teen years, the vast majority of those are not impacted over the long term. However, repeated exposure to ACEs in childhood and the teen years is much more frequent than anyone realized prior to this seminal study, showing again the need for all professionals to become more aware of and involved in finding and helping children exposed to extensive trauma. As noted earlier, the COVID-19 pandemic further exacerbated this concern.

The CDC (2021) provides questionnaires that are much more extensive than a mere list of these "Top 10 ACEs." Those questionnaires are available for both females and males, and clinicians may sometimes use data collected from them to help document exposure to ACEs in a client's early life. We do not recommend use of these types of questionnaires by teachers, though counselors in the school may find these extensive (and free) questionnaires useful in some cases. Also, teachers may find that utilizing these questionnaires in a self-examination can assist them in expanding their own understanding of the impact of trauma. To calculate a personal ACEs score, one simply tallies one point for each of the ACEs one experienced prior to the age of 18, and then adds those together to obtain a total score. Any score of four or more ACEs represents some cause for concern. However, we should quickly note that a high ACEs score is not a "terminal prognosis" of lifelong failure. Various factors, persons, and events in life can offset the impact of ACEs, and these resilience factors are discussed further in Chapter 5 and several other chapters.

CLASSROOMS IMPACTED BY CHILDREN EXPOSED TO TRAUMA

Class Behaviors of Children Exposed to Trauma

Teachers must now consider what types of classroom behaviors children who are frequently traumatized might display in the classroom. However, again, there are no easy answers, and children exposed to trauma may react to the same type of event in drastically different ways. For example, years of childhood sexual abuse may create a young girl or boy who engages in frequent, highly risky sexual behaviors with almost everyone. In contrast, another young person exposed to the same type and frequency of sexual abuse may seem to shut down completely and have virtually no sexual experiences, choosing to relate to no one on intimate terms. Years of exposure to any of these serious ACEs can result in self-imposed isolation, which prohibits an individual from attending school as a young adult or holding a steady job later in life. Persons exposed to trauma may even become bullies themselves, using their age or size to control others who are younger or smaller.

Behavioral manifestations in the classroom can be virtually any type of overt behavior problem. On the other extreme, a shy child who never seems to engage with anyone in the class, including the teacher, may be a victim of many ACEs over an extended period of time. With these disjointed potential responses to trauma noted, we can, at the very least, note a variety of additional indicators for teachers to look for in the classroom. These are presented in Box 1.5.

Box 1.5 Characteristics of children exposed to multiple trauma

- Never trust anyone
- Resist any physical closeness (hugs, etc.)
- Often show fierce pride
- Harsh judgments of self and others
- Rarely or never apologize (it shows weakness)
- Frequently excessively aggressive
- Never celebrate their own achievements
- Show little or no emotion
- Occasionally are explosively hostile
- Never request help
- Seek perfect fairness and resent unfairness
- Frequently refuse help when it is offered
- Often show discomfort in social situations
- Have limited or no friends

With all the "unknowns" discussed earlier, there are one or two certainties in serving students exposed to extended trauma. First of all, these students will require, if not demand, much more time and attention from the teacher than other students, including students with more commonly observed behavioral problems. With this in mind, we present in this book a variety of ways for teachers to prepare their class setting for students exposed to trauma, in advance of the arrival of the children themselves. This will take some preparation time prior to the beginning of the year, and may also require teachers to vary their preferred teaching style a bit. However, this is worth the effort in the long run, as the data show virtually all classrooms are likely to include one or more children exposed to repeated trauma. More of these general instructional guidelines and class preparation ideas are presented in Chapters 2, 3, and 4.

Next, children and teens exposed to six or more ACEs will usually require some type of counseling, in order to help process the things that have happened to them. While teachers may be the first to note problems or concerns for a given student, we urge all teachers to approach these issues carefully, and to always consult with a school counselor or school psychologist as soon as one suspects an ongoing trauma-based problem. Again, virtually all school districts today provide guidelines and, in some cases, forms and structured procedures for handling suspected dangerous situations, and teachers should become aware of, and implement, their district's policies for these instances.

The Need for Control

As practitioners, we have both worked fairly regularly with various individuals who were exposed to multiple traumas during childhood and adolescence. In one case, a young woman shared the following insights about her need for control in her world and related that need directly to trauma she had experienced as a child. No transcript was made of that talk at the time, but the following is a paraphrase of that highly informative discussion.

Vignette 1.6 Trauma and the need for control

Anyone who went through the hell I lived in will come out a control freak! You're writing a book on working with kids in trauma, right? Tell them that the single biggest issue for kids like me is control. Control is everything!

Imagine a fifth-grade student from a good family and that kid's response to being disciplined for something in class. That kid is probably used to being disciplined by her parents and maybe other adults (grandparents, coaches, church teachers, girl scout masters, etc.). All those adults are larger than the child, and the child probably believes that those adults are more knowledgeable about things, and that they have the child's best interest at heart. In short, because those kids feel the love of parents in a normal home and are generally secure, they will typically trust the adults more—trust them not to hurt them. For example, the night before that kid misbehaved in school, that child probably ate a meal at the family table, at which

(Continued)

Vignette 1.6 (Continued)

there were smiles, laughter, and love. Maybe the parents asked how the child's day went or what was going on in school. Some of us never had that, and we feel it every day! It's like something is missing.

Now imagine that same kid, same age and everything, but living the life I lived. Imagine how that child felt when punished by a teacher that she couldn't possibly trust. I was in seven different placements after the age of 13, including a number of foster families and a few group homes. Even before I left my mom's house, I remember some days when we didn't get to eat, or when my older brother and I would search the kitchen for anything we could find. Mom shouted a lot and spanked us sometimes. She wanted to hurt us. Mostly, though, she just let us be; she didn't have the time or the concern, not really. Sometimes, she didn't come home at night. I also remember Mom passed out from drug use in her bedroom, or entertaining some man in the bedroom. Any intrusion, in that case, resulted in us being screamed at and told to leave the room.

In that world, control is everything, and teachers don't really understand. How does that fifth grader, raised like I was, feel when a teacher disciplines her? We didn't understand that discipline could come from caring. Our world was dangerous, and we ran away from things that hurt. Our feelings were hurt all the time. We had to know when to leave Mom alone and go outside and play, and if it weren't for my brother, I could not have made it. Sometimes he made me bathe when I didn't remember to, and he helped me pick out my clothes before we went to catch the school bus. Sometimes we just hid from Mom, when she came in really late. I and my brother will always be control freaks because we had to be. We don't really trust anyone.

One more thing to tell teachers. If teachers understand how we need control, they can use that to teach us. If teachers could only understand this, they could influence kids like me. Give us control! Control over where we sit, or how we do our work. Choice in assignments, or how to complete my work, or any type of control helped me a lot, but most teachers didn't get that. I wanted to sit in the back because I was scared every time someone sat behind me. Also, teachers should point out to kids like me that getting a really good education will help them have more control over their lives in the long run. Like I said, control is everything! That's an important motivation, and teachers should use that.

This example speaks for itself. If teachers can get the sense of how important some control over one's environment is for students exposed to repeated trauma, they can then find ways to provide some degree of increased control for the child, depending on that child's age. This is one critical step, and an important place for teachers to begin, when seeking to establish trust with these children.

SO WHAT DO I DO IN THE CLASSROOM?

At this point, most teachers and clinicians will realize that working with children from very traumatic backgrounds is somewhat daunting, but we are still left with the major question: "What do I do with them?" The remainder of this book will give you many suggested approaches, and as a framework for those various tactics and home-use strategies, one might imagine a rather simple statement of goals: *We find them, we reach them, and then we teach them.*

Of course, the simplicity of this statement drastically misrepresents the challenges for teachers and counselors serving kids exposed to trauma. In finding these students, teachers must become aware of the types of sudden behavioral changes that may indicate various underlying trauma, either in the home or elsewhere. Once a child is identified as having suffered through various trauma, the teacher and counselor must find a way to reach them. Establishing some degree of trust with such a child or teen is even more challenging than establishing trust with other students who might demonstrate various types of behavioral problems. Finally, once a child is identified as needing some assistance because of trauma, and once a teacher and counselor have established some degree of mutual trust with that child, the teacher must still implement strategies focused on the curriculum at hand to teach the student.

Finding Them

Finding children who have experienced multiple ACEs in life is somewhat easier than either reaching them or teaching them. Many of these children exposed to extensive trauma will have been identified well before they begin their school years, whereas others, who may display behavior problems unlike other students or whose behavior may suddenly change, will be relatively easy to spot. In many cases, children who have experienced multiple traumas may already be seeing a counselor not associated with the school district, and in such cases, a close cooperation should be established between that counselor and the teacher and school counselor.

With that said, trauma may occur at any point in life, including after a child is placed in a particular grade or class, so teachers must be vigilant in watching for changing life circumstances or changes in children's behaviors that may indicate the beginning of a traumatic experience. In particular, trauma impacts different children in different ways, and teachers much note any significant changes in behavior.

We should also note that many children who experience abuse are "coached" by their abuser to not share their experiences with others outside the home. Thus, even teachers or other family members may be immediately excluded from the circle of trust of that child. The best practice, in these cases, is for the teacher to "trust one's feelings" about a child's behavioral changes, emotional state, or changing moods. Also, we urge teachers to write down and date their specific observations, sharing those with a counselor at school, and perhaps with the principal, depending on the school guidelines. Care should always be taken to not accuse anyone of anything in such notations, but rather write one's observations and note why they were of concern (and, of course, sign and date that observation). Again, various schools may have specific forms for this, and the school principal and counselor should be consulted immediately when any concern arises.

There is a two-faceted reality herein. Such notes are official documents and may show up in later court cases, though this is extremely rare. Thus, no one should be accused of anything, and no assumptions made, initially in these observation notes. On the other hand, it is not an overstatement to say that some children's lives have been saved from a nightmare of abuse because a vigilant teacher noted some concerns and shared them, in a professional and caring manner, with a counselor. Again, professionals should consult together, and then determine an appropriate course of action.

Reaching Them

Once a problem is documented, the teacher has the responsibility to reach the child and earn their trust. Of course, one might argue that this is the essence of teaching and counseling for almost all students, and while that is true, teachers and clinicians will find that this task is much more involved, and probably much more difficult, when children or teens have been traumatized. Teachers, of course, are not trained therapists and should not attempt "therapy" with these children. Such therapy is the role of the counselor or a private clinician, and each teacher must respect the limits of their training, and not exceed those limits.

With that stated, the elementary school child will typically spend 20–30 hours weekly with a teacher, whereas therapy takes place, typically, for one hour per week. Thus, it is possible, if not likely, that the teacher initially becomes closer to the child than a psychologist or counselor in cases in which counseling sessions are not taking place at all or are only just beginning. In those cases, a child may open up more with the teacher than with a clinician, if they open up at all.

For this reason, it is critical that teachers attempt to establish some level of trust with children who face the challenges of repeated trauma. Consistency during one's interactions with the child, along with openness, honesty, and a calm, measured response to every behavior the child exhibits, will go a long way to establishing trust. Teachers must demonstrate a willingness to talk openly with the child, in an ongoing effort to make the child feel comfortable. This will often take time outside the classroom. Of course, all of this becomes even more difficult if the child is openly challenging the teacher via inappropriate behavioral outbursts.

Finally, when it comes to reaching these kids and establishing some trust, teachers must realize that even very small things can represent huge successes with these deeply injured children and teens because they will tend to be so much more secretive than other children. As Vignette 1.6 indicated, both trust and control are giant issues for these students, and it will take time to establish any trust at all with these kids. Box 1.6 provides some additional guidelines for how teachers might proceed in this challenging task.

Box 1.6 Guidelines for reaching children exposed to trauma

- Learn more about all risk factors that cause trauma and their impact on children.
- Reflect on all behavioral concerns in the class, asking the question, "Is this 'normal' misbehavior, or does this represent a deeper problem?"
- Help kids exposed to trauma learn to take care of themselves. Talk about taking care of "yourself" in class. These kids must understand that it is okay to think about their own safety when faced with dangerous situations.

(Continued)

(Continued)

- Help kids exposed to trauma learn to have fun.
- Help deeply injured kids understand unconditional love.
- Talk about trust, good behavior, and rewards for good behavior.
- Talk with kids about dangers of risky behavior in an age-appropriate manner.
- Teach "appropriate" social media usage and limit screen time for this application.
- Help deeply injured kids and adolescents find support to share their experiences with others.

Teaching Them

Teaching these deeply traumatized students means moving them through the curriculum in such a way that they master the content while continuing to develop a trusting relationship with the teacher that allows for growing trust and increased control by the child over their environment. As former classroom teachers, we recognize the difficulty that any teacher would have in, on the one hand, observing behavioral problems manifested by these children and needing to effectively discipline them while, on the other hand, trying to find ways to discipline them *and* increase their sense of control simultaneously. Can anyone imagine a more difficult challenge? In some ways, these aims are diametrically opposed to each other, but no one said this would be either easy or comfortable.

What we can state is the importance of accomplishing this nearly impossible goal—developing a growing trusting relationship while effectively disciplining the child, increasing the child's sense of control, and leading the child through the curriculum. Only such a combination is likely to foster the child's growth, and once teachers have found ways to do all of these simultaneously, they truly have the hope of moving the child toward a more successful life. As in many aspects of teaching and counseling, the task is difficult, but the rewards can be huge, both for the child and for the teacher.

Thus, finding teaching activities that allow some student choice, along with increased openness and trust, should guide the overall teaching process. Box 1.7 lists some specific classroom needs that deeply injured kids have, and most of these suggest specific ideas for teaching that can be accomplished with some extra time and work by a caring classroom teacher.

Box 1.7 Classroom needs of children exposed to trauma

- Consistency in disciplinary policies
- Written, posted rules to follow, developed with the input of the children in the class
- Consistent consequences for misbehavior
- Choices of assignments to allow these children some control in the classroom
- Choices among punishments, as possible
- A highly structured daily plan and work schedule with only a few essential variations
- Clear work expectations from the teacher
- Explicit, directive communications from the teacher
- Classwide and one-to-one discussions on disciplinary issues
- A firm, fair, businesslike (i.e., nonemotional) approach to issues that arise in class
- Time (and a strategy) to help students calm themselves after a problem arises
- A genuineness from the teacher, which will help establish mutual trust
- A willingness from the teacher to talk with these challenged kids as problems arise
- A private communication mechanism between teacher and student, such as hand signals or journal entries, to facilitate open but private communication
- A degree of sensitivity when critiquing a child's schoolwork
- A willingness to make exceptions for students challenged by repeated trauma

SUMMARY

As this chapter has shown, nearly 50% of all children are exposed to trauma before their 18th birthday, and in most cases these children recover from such exposure and generally do well in life thereafter. However, children exposed to four or more of the highly impactful ACEs may be considered to have been repeatedly traumatized, and in cases in which such trauma is long-term, these students are likely to present challenges in the classroom and may show a wide variety of challenging and risky behaviors throughout life. Further, a wide variety of mental and physical health issues are likely to arise among these students, and clearly they will act and respond differently than other children in the classroom.

In response, teachers and clinicians must identify these students, reach them by establishing some level of mutual trust, and then teach them. A number of indicators of various types of ACEs have been presented, and while clinicians are typically aware of these issues, some teachers may not be. This chapter has also presented some general teaching guidelines for instructional planning and for interactions with these children, which should help teachers in managing these students in the classroom.

With that noted, traumatized children and adolescents will need much more attention and time than other students in the class, including other students who manifest behavioral problems. For most deeply injured children, some type of therapy will likely be needed, and teachers must keep the counselor or therapist informed about changes in behavior, mood, or emotions shown by these students. At times, troubled children and teens may be receiving medications for some of these problems; SSRIs are quite commonly prescribed for anxiety/depression, as one example. Teachers will need to closely monitor the impact of these treatments on each student's work and behavior in the classroom, and to keep the counselors or physicians informed of all relevant behavioral changes.

The teaching guidelines presented in this chapter are only the beginning point for instruction. The next three chapters will describe how teachers should construct the teaching environment to facilitate effective teaching for these students, and many more guidelines are provided therein. Further, the remaining chapters present a number of specific teaching strategies that are much more involved and can greatly assist these students in the classroom and even in the home environment. In this book, we use the term *teaching guideline* when an idea or suggestion can be summed up in one or two sentences, whereas the term *teaching strategy* is used to represent a more involved instructional intervention for students exposed to multiple traumas. Thus, Chapters 2, 3, and 4 are filled with many more teaching guidelines for consideration by all teachers and clinicians, while each subsequent chapter of the book presents one specific teaching strategy or intervention approach teachers can utilize, along with detailed instructions on implementation.

In some cases, parents working with a teacher or therapist can likewise implement these teaching guidelines and strategies (e.g., mindfulness, avoidance of triggers, or use of emotional support animals). In such cases, the use of a particular strategy by parents will be mentioned in the chapter. Teachers should feel free to consider any and all of the teaching strategies herein and implement one or two of these strategies that most closely align with the needs of the student, their teaching situation, and their teaching style.

With that noted, we do urge teachers to implement *something* for students who are victims of repeated or extensive trauma. With perhaps 16%–20% of all children exposed to repeated trauma, most classes will include one, two, or more of these students, so schools simply must do more to address the needs of these kids exposed to trauma. Further, no educator or school-based clinician should believe that the general guidelines in Box 1.7 or in the next several chapters are "enough." Rather, all schools should immediately consider the specific, highly involved instructional strategy interventions presented in subsequent chapters here, and select the one, or two, or three that seem to be the best fit. Some of these (e.g., mindfulness, adult mentoring, and restorative justice) may best be implemented schoolwide, whereas individual teachers may take the lead in implementing others, as needed.

What we can say with certainty is that, absent some implementation of these strategies for children who are victims of extensive or repeated trauma, instruction will be quite tenuous, and positive lifelong outcomes for the child will be in grave doubt. Clearly, that is a result that no educator or clinician will be able to live with.

REFERENCES

ABC15 Arizona. (2018, June 8). *Centers for Disease Control: Suicides rates have increased 30 percent since 1999.* Retrieved from https://www.abc15.com/news/region-northeast-valley/scottsdale/centers-for-disease-control-suicides-rates-have-increased-30-percent-since-1999

Adams, J. M. (2013, December 2). Schools promoting "trauma-informed" teaching to reach troubled students. *EdSource.* Retrieved from https://edsource.org/2013/schools-focus-on-trauma-informed-to-reach-troubled-students/51819

American Addiction Centers. (2022, September 9). *Children of addicted parents guide: How to deal with addict parents.* Retrieved from https://americanaddictioncenters.org/guide-for-children/

Annie E. Casey Foundation. (2023, January 19). *Nearly 11 million kids face food insecurity as statistic dips to 20-year low.* Retrieved from https://aecf.org/blog/nearly-11-million-kids-face-food-insecurity-as-statistic-dips-to-20-year-low

Anxiety and Depression Association of America. (2021, February 19). *Anxiety and depression in children.* Retrieved from https://adaa.org/living-with-anxiety/children/anxiety-and-depression

Centers for Disease Control and Prevention. (2021, April 6). *About the CDC-Kaiser ACE study*. Retrieved from https://www.cdc.gov/violence prevention/aces/about.html

Centers for Disease Control and Prevention. (2022, April 6). *Fast facts: Preventing child abuse and neglect*. Retrieved from https://www.cdc.gov/ violenceprevention/childabuseandneglect/fastfact.html

Centers for Disease Control and Prevention. (2023). *Suicide data and statistics*. Retrieved from https://www.cdc.gov/suicide/suicide-data-statistics.html

Conklin, A. (2023, September 4). Social media giants like TikTok, YouTube, fuel "youth mental health crisis" school boards claim in lawsuit. *Fox News*. Retrieved from foxnews.com/us/social-media-giants-like-TikTok-YouTube-fuel-youth-mental-health-crisis-school-boards-claim-lawsuit

Creamer, J., Shrider, E. A., Burns, K., & Chen, F. (2022, September 13). *Poverty in the United States: 2021* (Report Number P60-277). U.S. Census Bureau. Retrieved from https://www.census.gov/library/publications/2022/demo/ p60-277.html

Felitti, V., & Anda, R. (2009). *The adverse childhood experiences (ACE) study: Bridging the gap between childhood traumas and negative consequences later in life*. Retrieved from www.acestudy.org

Felitti, V., Anda, R. F., Nordenberg, D., Williamson, D. F., Spitz, A. M., Edwards, V., & Marks, J. S. (1998). Relationship of childhood abuse and household dysfunction to many of the leading causes of death in adults. *American Journal of Preventive Medicine, 14*, 245–258.

Ivey-Stephenson, A., Demissie, Z., Crosby, A. E., Stone, D. M., Gaylor, M. P. H., Wilkins, N., . . . Brown, M. (2023). *Suicidal ideation and behaviors among high school students—Youth Risk Behavior Survey, United States, 2019*. Centers for Disease Control and Prevention. Retrieved from https://www.cdc.gov/ mmwr/volumes/69/su/su6901a6.htm

Morin, A. (2023, November 20). *Understanding the effects of childhood trauma*. Verywell Mind. Retrieved from https://www.verywellmind.com/what-are-the-effects-of-childhood-trauma-4147640

National Center for Victims of Crime. (2023). *Child sexual abuse statistics*. Retrieved from https://victimsofcrime.org/child-sexual-abuse-statistics/

National Children's Alliance. (2023). *National statistics on child abuse*. Retrieved from https://www.nationalchildrensalliance.org/media-room/national-stati stics-on-child-abuse/

National Institute on Drug Abuse. (n.d.). *Parents and educators*. Retrieved from https://nida.nih.gov/research-topics/parents-educators

National Institutes of Health. (2018, July 10). *Treatment for depression in young children*. Retrieved from https://www.nih.gov/news-events/nih-research-matters/treatment-depression-young-children

Newsmax. (2023). US suicides hit an all-time high last year. Retrieved from https://newsmax.com/health/health-news/suicide-record-2022-guns/2023/08/10/id/1130341

Quirk, M. (2023, February 9). The benefits of mindfulness education in schools. *Psychology Today*. Retrieved from https://www.psychologytoday.com/us/blog/evidence-based-living/202302/the-benefits-of-mindfulness-education-in-schools

Reinberg, S. (2021, August 10). *Pandemic has depression and anxiety rising globally among young people, data shows*. United Press International. Retrieved from https://www.upi.com/Health_News/2021/08/10/Pandemic-has-depression-anxiety-rising-globally-among-young-people-data-shows/1411628541635/

Rind, B., Tromovitch, P., & Bauserman, R. (1998). A meta-analytic examination of assumed properties of child sexual abuse using college samples. *Psychological Bulletin, 124*(1), 22–53.

Rosenthal, M. (2021). Intergenerational Trauma: An Embodied Experience. *International Body Psychotherapy Journal, 20*(2), 80–86.

Scott, C. F., Marcu, G., Anderson, R. E., Newman, M. W., & Schoenebeck, S. (2023, February 10). *Trauma-informed social media: Towards solutions for reducing and healing online harm*. Cornell University. Retrieved from https://arxiv.org/abs/2302.05312

Sporleder, J., & Forbes, H. T. (2016). *The trauma-informed school: A step-by-step implementation guide for administrators and school personnel*. Beyond Consequences Institute.

Timmen, L., & Cermack, M. D. (1985). *A primer on adult children of alcoholics*. Health Communications.

U.S. Administration for Children and Families. (2023, June 27). *Child maltreatment*. U.S. Department of Health and Human Services. Retrieved from https://www.acf.hhs.gov/cb/data-research/child-maltreatment

U.S. Department of Veterans Affairs. (2022, September 22). *How common is PTSD in children and teens?* Retrieved from https://www.ptsd.va.gov/understand/common/common_children_teens.asp

Whealin, J., & Barnett, E. (2007, May 22). *Child sexual abuse*. U.S. Department of Veterans Affairs. National Center for Posttraumatic Stress Disorder.

CHAPTER 2

CLASSROOM BASICS FOR STUDENTS EXPOSED TO TRAUMA

As noted throughout Chapter 1, one in every five students has been challenged by exposure to multiple adverse childhood experiences, or ACEs (Centers for Disease Control and Prevention, 2020; Felitti & Anda, 2009; Quirk, 2023; Reinberg, 2021), and these data suggest that virtually every public school classroom includes at least one of these students. Therefore, teachers and clinicians must be prepared to deal effectively with students exposed to multiple traumas. This involves many things, but initially, teachers must prepare their classes to receive these students. Further, both teachers and the kids themselves, as their age allows, need to understand trauma and how trauma impacts students. Such understanding can be critical to any efforts to improve the children's mental health, as well as academic performance. The relatively new term *trauma-informed* is used to describe teachers and school faculties who have received some training in trauma awareness, and schools in which students are taught to prepare for, survive, and emotionally deal with trauma (Adams, 2014; Cole et al., 2005; Lippman & Schmitz, 2013; Simmons-Duffin, 2018). To get an immediate picture of a trauma-informed school, we suggest that readers review one of the brief YouTube videos on schools preparing themselves for trauma, and several we recommend may be found on the companion website for this book (https://traumahelpnow.com).

This chapter begins with brain functioning, because that discussion will help teachers and clinicians understand more about the needs of students exposed to multiple ACEs. This includes information on how to prepare students at various ages to understand how their brain functions and how trauma may impact their brain functioning. This instruction will, of necessity, be age dependent, but in many schools even primary-grade children are taught a bit about brain functioning and how trauma may impact the brain. Such knowledge can assist even very young children to explore and to some degree self-regulate their emotions, moods, and behaviors.

Both the remainder of this chapter and the next two chapters will focus on preparing the classroom for students exposed to multiple ACEs. Finally, every remaining chapter in this book will focus on one specific intervention that will help teachers, clinicians, and in many cases parents address the needs of these children and teens. Each of these emphases is a critical focus of the trauma-informed school: knowing the indicators of various traumas, preparing classrooms appropriately, teaching about brain functioning, and implementing targeted intervention strategies focused on helping children individually begin to master their personal issues.

TRAUMA AND BRAIN FUNCTIONING

Beyond recognizing trauma indicators, the next step in becoming a trauma-informed school is developing understanding of brain functioning and how childhood trauma may impact brain functioning (Craig, 2017; Perry, 2014). The human brain is a marvelous instrument and is wonderfully designed to change itself throughout life. Further, each change is either genetically or environmentally driven, so it is clear that a child's brain will, to a large degree, reflect the world in which the child has been raised (Doidge, 2007). If the child's world is characterized by violence, verbal threats, abuse, unpredictability, fear, and other ACEs, their brain will reflect that by altering the development of the neural systems involved in the stress, aggression, and fear responses (Chemtob, Novaco, Hamada, Gross, & Smith, 1997; Craig, 2017; Eller & Hierck, 2021; Perry, 2000). In short, some children's brains have literally become "wired by trauma," and this can result in different-sized brain regions for some students who experience repeated trauma.

Of course, brain development and brain functioning go hand in hand, and both begin in the womb. Further, human brains are even more sensitive to, and reactive to, their environment at young ages. The fact that some very young children are frequently exposed to trauma will alter brain development, which in turn will impact both brain functioning and behavior at early ages and, in most cases, many years later (Doidge, 2007; Lebow, 2021). For example, the amygdala is an area in the lower brain that interprets sensory data, and seeks threats in order to protect the young child. This is the primary brain area that hosts the survival instinct of "fight, flight, or freeze," and for children exposed to repeated trauma, this area becomes much larger and generally much more active. Because it is one of the earliest brain areas to develop, it is impacted by early trauma, even prior to the full development of other brain areas. Thus, children exposed to multiple ACEs from an early age typically engage the fight, flight, or freeze response much more frequently than do other children.

Further, childhood trauma may impact the young brain even before language is developed, and thus, these children during the later school years are less than capable when it comes to expressing themselves about certain fears, behaviors, events, or situations that they perceive as related to an earlier traumatic insult (Cole et al., 2005; Craig, 2017; Osofsky, 2019). Also, either the right or the left hemisphere of the brain may be differentially impacted by childhood insult (Craig, 2017). This may add to the inability of a child to answer certain questions like "Why did you do that?" or "What's wrong?" simply because that child's language had not yet been developed when their brain was first repeatedly exposed to trauma. Hasn't virtually every veteran teacher been confronted with a situation in which a child was asked a question along these lines, only to be confronted with a child who is, seemingly, incapable of answering? This frequently results when the left hemisphere (where language is typically localized in the brain) is impacted by trauma prior to the development of language (Craig, 2017; Osofsky, 2019).

While extensive understanding of brain functioning is not a reasonable expectation for teachers or school counselors, having some insight into how a traumatized child's brain may respond can help these professionals understand why children do what they do, particularly when their responses seem to be far outside the norm (Craig, 2017; Eller & Hierck, 2021). To illustrate several possible impacts of trauma on children's brains, Box 2.1 presents some examples of traumatic brain insults and later behavior patterns that might logically be associated with them.

Box 2.1 Brain trauma and related school behaviors

Examples of childhood trauma	Aberrant classroom behaviors
Child suffers physical abuse to left hemisphere before age 2 when language develops. Neutral connections associated with violence are made before child can speak.	Child hits another kid in Grade 4, and teacher asks, "Why did you do that?" Child cannot answer. They have no verbal memory to answer (Craig, 2017). For that child, hitting may be a preverbal response, based on how the brain was impacted before language developed.
Child is exposed to sexual abuse from age 5 until 14. Neural connections develop that connect physical proximity with fear and pain.	Anytime someone is behind or near them, child flinches or shows fear. Child may hit or show aggression whenever someone gets too close.
Child is in a car accident that damages the hippocampus, which increases the stress hormone glucocorticoid. This might kill the brain cells associated with memory connections.	Child might hear screaming car tires, or a car horn, and jump under the desk for safety, not realizing the real threat is long past (Lebow, 2021).
Child is fearful of abuse at home. Sympathetic nervous system is highly activated, resulting in an elevation of hormones associated with stress, and possible lack of sleep.	Child frequently seems tired and falls asleep in class nearly every day. They are hard to wake up (Lebow, 2021) and may be terrified of sleeping at home.

TEACHING STUDENTS ABOUT THE BRAIN

Of course, in addition to ensuring that teachers know a bit about brain functioning and how trauma may impact thinking or behavior, trauma-informed teachers are teaching the fundamentals of brain functioning to children from the lower elementary years through high school (Craig, 2017; Lebow, 2021). This instruction can empower children to correctly understand events that they may otherwise perceive as threats, and thus, they will begin to respond differently in the classroom. This instruction is likely to help decrease aggression and overt violence in some children over time. Several general understandings about brain functioning can help in this regard, and each is described in this section.

The Three-Part Brain and Brain Function

Using the concept of the brain's three major functional areas, teachers should initially teach children a bit about how their brains function, how trauma may impact their brains, and how those brain functions impact their own thoughts and behaviors (Craig, 2017; Lebow, 2021). A simple explanation of brain functioning is the triune brain, presented in Box 2.2. Although this model of brain functioning has recently been challenged as somewhat inaccurate or overly simplistic (Steffen, Hedges, & Matheson, 2022), it has become the most frequently used model for explaining basic brain functions to children and teenagers.

Box 2.2 The triune brain

The **reptilian brain** (the term *lizard brain* is often used with younger children) refers to the lower level of the brain and brain stem, and this innermost part of the brain matures first. This is a brain component that humans have in common with reptiles, and while reptiles do not have other higher-functioning brain areas, mammals do. Still, this brain section is responsible for survival instincts, aggression, and automatic body processes (e.g., heart beating and breathing without having to think about it). Most sensory data are initially analyzed by this part of the brain, and this survival mechanism allows for responses to perceived danger even prior to a rational "thought" of danger in other brain areas. In fact, this brain area always searches for danger (as do reptiles) and, when any threat is perceived, essentially takes over our emotions, our body, and our behavior completely. In evolutionary terms, this helped ensure our survival. Most aggressive behavior and all instinctual behavior stems from this brain component.

Children who were traumatized early in life probably developed nearly "automatic" behaviors concerning how to interact with the world and react to threats using mainly this brain region. That is because this region was more developed when the early trauma occurred. Thus, these kids tend to be much more aggressive than normal, and they tend to believe that such aggression is normal. They perceive threats virtually everywhere and typically respond with a "lizard-brained" fight, flight, or freeze response, and as a result, they may appear to misbehave much more frequently than other children. For students exposed to trauma, such behavior may have been optimal, in some ways protecting them from abuse, in the home environment.

The **midbrain** (limbic system or emotional brain) is the midlevel area of the brain, which processes emotions. The limbic system, associated with social and

(Continued)

(Continued)

nurturing behaviors and mutual reciprocity, conveys sensory data. Older students might also be taught about the amygdala, the part of the limbic system that scans for threats and controls emotions by tagging senses, memories, emotions, and behavior together. In situations of perceived danger, the amygdala sends a "danger" signal to the lizard brain using the hormone cortisol. Then, that lower level of the brain takes over to ensure survival of the organism. Thus, in situations of perceived danger, the lizard brain effectively hijacks other brain functions, and higher-level functions such as rational thought or problem solving stop (Eller & Hierck, 2021). At that point, a child is in full "survival mode." Children exposed to trauma constantly may be caught up in this hijacking and, as we've noted before, may perceive as threats many things that are not threats, thus activating the fight, flight, or freeze response and eliciting aggressive and/ or defensive behavior.

The **forebrain and neocortex** (the term *smart part* may be used for younger children) is the most highly evolved part of the brain, and this brain region controls our language, thinking, cognitive processing, planning, decision making, reflection, reasoned judgment, and learning. Although functional from an early age, this part of the brain matures completely only in the young adult years (aged 22 through 24). Learning to use these brain functions in times of stress, fear, or perceived threat frees us from exclusive use of the reptile brain and generally helps us make better decisions. Thus, students should be taught to move away from aggressive behavior by using their "smart part." For example, when verbally "attacked" by a classmate, even very young children can be taught to use their smart part to talk to themselves, saying, "I'm angry [or hurt], so I should take a deep breath and then leave this area instead of hitting back." Thus, using the smart part helps that child avoid their lizard brain desire to fight back.

In teaching about these brain parts, teachers might point out that the reptilian (or lizard) brain controls our survival instincts—such as the famed fight, flight, or freeze response (Eller & Hierck, 2021). When children exposed to trauma seem more aggressive than their classmates, it is usually because their lizard brain has taken control. In the context of the classroom, we should teach all children that instead of being controlled by the lizard brain, we can use other sections of our brain—such as our forebrain and neocortex, or smart part—to "talk to ourselves" when we feel angry or anxious, and then we can often choose a better course of action. Even young kids can understand that talking themselves out of being angry will help them get into much less trouble, and the following YouTube video provides an example of this instruction:

https://bit.ly/3uKIDeG

To read a QR code, you must have a smartphone or tablet with a camera. We recommend that you download a QR code reader app that is made specifically for your phone or tablet brand.

We urge teachers to use this video (or similar videos discussed on the companion website for this book: https://traumahelpnow.com) in their classrooms to teach children about brain functioning, from the primary grades and up.

NEURONS THAT FIRE TOGETHER WIRE TOGETHER

Next, teachers should teach that habitual behavior stems from frequently repeated past experiences coupled with how a child responded to those experiences. One commonly noted wisdom used by brain researchers is the old adage "Neurons that fire together wire together!" That means that sets of neurons firing together will increase the likelihood of the same neuronal set firing together again (or "wiring together"). This frequent, repetitive pattern then forms a "go-to" brain response. Numerous previous experiences of the same type of situation elicit the same neurons firing together, or the same neuronal brain activity (Craig, 2017). Therefore, experiences of abuse (e.g., being hit or verbally attacked) will typically partner with (i.e., wire together) a behavioral response of either aggression or running away.

For example, imagine a complex set of perhaps a million or two million neurons firing together each time a child is physically hit prior to the age of 2. Trauma early in life will typically cause some delay in language development (Osofsky, 2019; Rosenthal, 2021), so at that age the child will have virtually no expressive language and limited cognitive thought processes. Nevertheless, the lizard brain—the only brain part close to maturity at this point—is learning behavioral responses to being hit. Those neuronal firings might dictate a nonverbal thought in the child's brain that goes something like this: "I've been hit—I should run away or hit back!" Of course, that single thought can easily mutate into something like "I might be hit; I should hit back now!" Each of these thoughts would take place in the lowest level of the child's brain—the survival level or the lizard brain. Still, if that child was exposed to repeated physical violence at a very young age, then that particular neuronal set may well be so strongly connected (i.e., wired together) that the child displays the same aggressive and/or hitting behavior whenever they feel threatened in any way in the classroom many years later. This is why many students exposed to multiple traumas are so aggressive.

Alternatively, for some students, their particular neuronal wiring may have paired the abuse they experienced with a neuronal response of "hide" or "run." Those children will manifest behaviors of quiet withdrawal, extreme shyness, and, in some cases, extremely poor social skills.

Constant, frequent violent trauma yields consistent brain responses, and often, consistent violent experiences and those brain responses become hardwired over time. The resulting aggression (or extreme withdrawal) can easily show up many years later, when a child is 10 or 15, in response to any perceived threat, whether real or imagined! In many cases, the child's aggression or withdrawal will seem to be entirely out of proportion to the circumstances. Teachers must understand that troubled kids do not need to actually be hit for that set of neuronal connections to fire. Rather, the child merely needs to *perceive* a possible threat of violence, and they will then begin one or another set of these neuronal responses. Any perceived threat may elicit this reaction from such a child.

Again, when a child, particularly a child widely exposed to trauma, feels threatened, the lizard brain takes total control, shutting down other brain functions and shifting the brain and body into a reactive, fight, flight, or freeze mode (Lebow, 2021; Osofsky, 2019; Perry, 2014). This scenario can, and often does, lead to out-of-control behaviors in the classroom. For this reason, teachers simply must strive to teach children exposed to trauma to use the smart part of their brain and thus activate other, higher brain functions, which can then be activated whenever a threat is perceived.

Neuroplasticity

Neuroplasticity is the concept that brain connections are malleable over time. Thus, an injured brain can "heal" itself; it is "plastic" and can, with practice, develop new neuron connections to represent more mature responses and more advanced learning (Doidge, 2007; Osofsky, 2019). In short, brains can "unlearn" old neuronal firing patterns created at earlier ages, and make new ones, a feat that was once thought impossible! Indeed, it was once believed that neuronal connections, once established, were virtually fixed for life, but brain research over recent decades has helped scientists discard that antiquated notion (Doidge, 2007; Lebow, 2021). Brain functions are amazingly malleable, and new learning, represented by new neuronal connections (i.e., new sets of neurons wired together), can be developed at any point throughout life. This is a very optimistic reality, particularly for students exposed to repeated trauma.

For children and adolescents exposed to drug addictions, childhood trauma, or other ACEs, this rewiring of the brain can be a long, arduous task. Still, it should be stressed that brains can and do recover from many types of traumatic insult (Doidge, 2007; Lebow, 2021). New neutral connections can be formed, and new behaviors in response to threats or perceived threats can be learned. This aspect of brain research should be emphasized strongly to children exposed to trauma, because the concept of neuroplasticity represents the hope of new behavioral habits; that is, children exposed to trauma can learn new brain connections that allow them to function in a more mature manner (Doidge, 2007). We simply must let students of trauma know that choosing to use the "smart part" of their brains will strengthen their more mature neuronal connections over time, and this will help them stay in control of themselves much better, be happier generally, and thus stay out of trouble. This is the very essence of brain-based, self-regulation of behavior.

Teach What Trauma Does to a Brain

In an age-appropriate way, trauma-informed teachers should teach these kids about how trauma impacts their own brains. As one might imagine, this must be done with great sensitivity because this will involve initially teaching children that their brains are "wired" somewhat differently from the brains of other students. For children who have been repeatedly traumatized, teachers should, carefully and with great sensitivity, help them understand that their brains are, to a degree, "programmed" for aggression and violent behavior, and that this is quite different from other children. Teachers must let students exposed to trauma know that this "wiring based on trauma" probably explains why they sometimes feel different, or maybe even why they seem to get into trouble at school more often than other kids. In this discussion, teachers and clinicians should quickly emphasize the good news that students *can* learn to use their smart part and thus develop increased control over their own moods and emotions.

Kids may respond either negatively or favorably to this type of lesson, and clearly this can be a very sensitive topic. Because this knowledge can potentially hurt or embarrass some children, this matter must be managed very carefully. We recommend that teachers and clinicians teach the entire class about brain functioning and then offer additional instruction to children exposed to trauma privately, in one-to-one situations. Teachers must use extreme caution here, but with that need for caution noted, it is, nevertheless, very important to hold such a discussion. Many students exposed to trauma know very well that they frequently have different responses and perspectives from their peers, and that will not typically come as a surprise to them. In fact, many of these students are already wondering, "Why am I different? Is something wrong with me?" Thus, this discussion may yield a very positive answer to those questions, and often makes these children feel better about themselves.

In working with both traumatized kids and adults, we have heard this same question quite often, and providing an accurate, scientific answer very often puts these individuals at ease. Again, this discussion must heavily emphasize the "good news" that brains can and will learn to rewire themselves as they increasingly experience safe, peaceful life situations and develop self-regulation over their moods and emotions. In fact, for some kids exposed to multiple ACEs, this discussion can be the very moment that turns their life around. A teacher or clinician can begin this discussion on trauma impacting the brain, by saying something like the following:

> Because of what you've gone through in life, you might see things differently than some other people, and this might cause your brain to react differently. Sometimes you might be more likely to fight or get angry than others, because that is what your brain is used to doing. Your lizard brain may have learned early that hitting back helped protect you at home, even though it doesn't work at school. That might be the reason you get into trouble a lot. Still, your brain is always changing and responding to the circumstances in your life, just like it should.

> The good news is that, as things get more and more peaceful for you here in school, you will learn to control your lizard brain feelings without hitting someone when you are angry. This can happen by learning to talk to yourself, take a deep breath, and then leave the situation. Your brain can learn to do that when you are angry or when your feelings get hurt. You know that you are safe here at school, and in fact, I think your brain is doing that right now, so all in all, your brain is doing just great! I'm proud of you for that!

When the question "Why am I different?" or "Why am I angry all the time?" is handled in that fashion, most students will understand that they can learn to behave in a way in which they do not feel such persistent aloneness or constant anger, and consequently they won't get into trouble as frequently. For many students, this is nothing less than a critical lifeline to a much-improved life!

WHAT ELSE DO TRAUMA-INFORMED SCHOOLS DO?

At this point, we've mentioned several things that schools should due to become trauma-informed schools:

- ▶ Preparing teachers to understand the warning signs for various types of childhood trauma
- ▶ Ensuring that teachers are informed about the impact of childhood trauma on behavior
- ▶ Helping teachers teach kids about traumatized brains, with great care and sensitivity
- ▶ Assisting teachers to set up their classrooms with students exposed to ACEs in mind
- ▶ Ensuring that teachers teach challenged kids that they can control their moods and emotions

In addition to these practices, trauma-informed schools tend to practice teaching approaches that are more appropriate for children exposed to trauma than are traditional classrooms (Craig, 2017). A few of these teaching tips are described in the following section, and many others are included in subsequent chapters.

Offer Students Choices

As noted previously, having some sense of control is critical for students exposed to trauma, and teachers can foster a sense of control over one's environment by offering choices whenever possible. Teachers have long realized that providing choices of assignments helps elicit more compliance and harder work from many students. However, for children exposed to multiple traumas, who very often sense that they have little control overall, such choices can have a much more positive impact (Perry, 2014). Choices of seating, of peer buddies in class, or among assignments, as well as other choices in school, will tend to increase a child's sense of self-control and typically will result in improved behavior in the classroom (Perry, 2014).

Perry (2014) also recommends structuring disciplinary consequences as choices for kids exposed to trauma. When a child is noncompliant, the teacher should frame the ensuing consequence as a choice to be made by the student. The teacher might say something like "You have a choice. You can choose to do what I have asked, or you can choose to lose five minutes of your recess time [or another negative consequence]. What would you like to choose?" Framing the interaction as a choice gives the student some sense of control, even in a situation requiring some discipline, and it might even help defuse a negative situation.

Emphasize Organizational Thinking

The child exposed to trauma quite often tends to be more disorganized than others in general (Adams, 2014; Craig, 2017; Lebow, 2021). For many deeply injured kids, the chaos and/or violence of their childhood probably seemed totally out of their control and entirely haphazard. For most of these kids, there was no development of any sense of cause and effect, or any ability to predict violence, in their chaotic home. For this reason, children exposed to trauma may not grasp these organizational concepts as quickly or as easily as other children (Craig, 2017).

Craig (2017) emphasizes the need to teach organizational skills, and the ability to internally organize knowledge. Of course, these same practices are, in most cases, best practices for all students, but they are more important for students exposed to repeated trauma. Teaching activities that stress organizational concepts such as estimation, prediction, patterns, or cause and effect, as well as reflective thinking at the end of a lesson, should be used whenever possible. Students need to develop the ability to understand and order knowledge internally, and this will take more work with kids exposed to trauma than with others (Craig, 2017).

Use Questions That Stress Organization and Brain Functioning

Also, the teacher may emphasize such organizational thinking even when no specific prediction or estimation activity is planned, merely by using appropriate question strategies (Craig, 2017). In a history lesson, for example, the teacher might ask about cause and effect or motivation by saying something like "Why do you think George Washington decided to cross the Delaware River and attack the British on Christmas Day? What did General Washington hope to accomplish with that attack, and did he succeed?" These questions should elicit the type of cause-and-effect thinking that students exposed to trauma need, since Washington's crossing did result both in a badly needed Patriot victory and in the reenlistment of many soldiers in his army.

Further, Craig (2017) suggests that once we teach kids about brain functions, we should emphasize brain functions throughout our academic lessons. In the preceding example, the teacher could continue the questioning about Washington by saying, "Okay, when General Washington decided to go ahead with that attack, did he make that decision quickly and impulsively, with his lizard brain, or did he think about it and make a smart part decision? What part of his brain helped him make that decision to attack that night?" Teachers can then point out that Washington, if nothing else, was quite deliberate in his actions in that instance, and he carefully considered the need for a victory to motivate the population and to encourage his soldiers to reenlist.

Teach Using Movement

In response to the emphasis on brain-compatible instruction over the last two decades, the importance of movement has been stressed for classrooms across the grade levels (Bender, 2012; Sousa, 2009). Movement has long been recommended as a teaching tool in elementary classes, and many examples are provided in the literature. Thus, most teachers today are using movement to represent academic concepts in the curriculum from kindergarten through elementary school. Further, numerous proponents have provided examples of movement-based instruction in middle and high school classes (Bender, 2012; Sousa, 2009).

However, in this context, we must point out that children exposed to trauma tend to respond very positively to movement-based instruction (Craig, 2017). Movement can have a calming effect for these students. Thus, movement-based teaching will help children who tend to be overly stressed anyway to relax more easily in the school environment.

CASE STUDY: KALIE'S AGGRESSIVE OUTBURSTS

Kalie was living in a foster placement, and had been for the previous two years, because her family home was dominated by her mother's ongoing drug addiction. Like many fourth graders who have been exposed to repeated trauma, Kalie demonstrated high levels of aggression, cursing, and occasional violence in class. Ms. Haygood, her teacher, believed that Kalie used aggression whenever she felt a loss of control or threatened, which, because of her background, was virtually every day. Ms. Haygood had already taught the class a bit about their brain functioning as described previously, so, in addition, she decided to implement an intervention for Kalie based on increasing the choices Kalie could make in assignments or other choices that she could offer Kalie during the school day. First, Ms. Haygood discreetly counted the violent outbursts, cursing episodes, and aggressive statements toward others made by Kalie. These data are presented in Figure 2.1.

As a second step, Ms. Haygood identified several choices that she could offer Kalie each day, based on variations in assignments, using the computer to complete work when possible, or choices of where to sit when doing a work period. Next, Ms. Haygood selected three other students who had manifested some mild behavior problems and explained to the class that she wanted to do an experiment with those four students. The experiment would involve how choices in the class might help students concentrate on their work better and behave better. Ms. Haygood then told the students that if the experiment worked, she would begin offering assignment choices and other choices to all the students as much as possible. This "multiple students" approach, and the promise that all

Figure 2.1 • *Violent or aggressive outbursts*

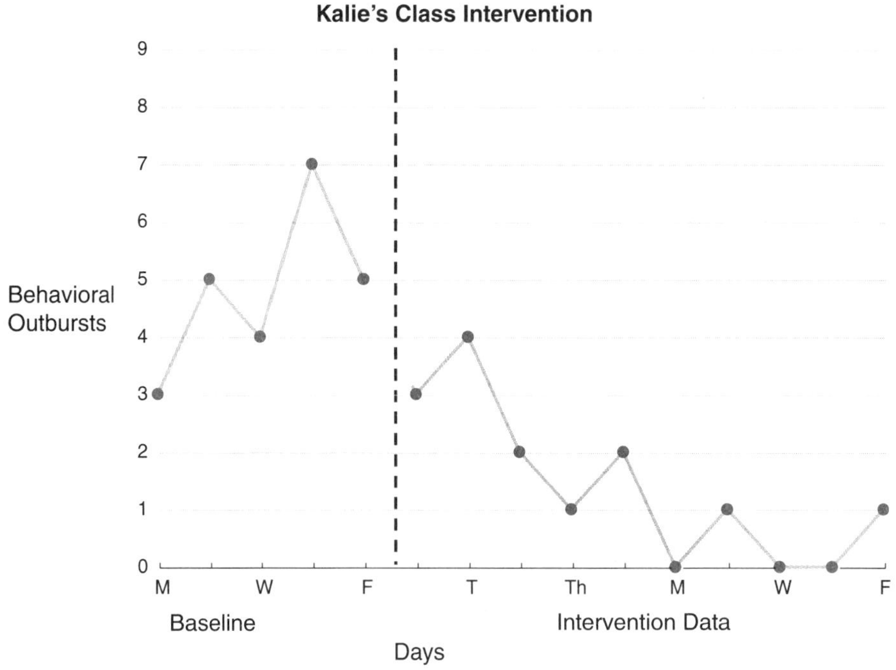

Kalie's Class Intervention

students might ultimately benefit, prevented any potential individual identification of Kalie as the target student for the experiment.

As the experiment progressed, Ms. Haygood found that with only minimal planning, she could develop varied assignments and offer options to the four students in the experiment. In many cases, the same differentiated assignments worked for all four students. However, she tallied only the aggression of Kalie, and as the data in Figure 2.1 indicate, the aggressive behaviors of Kalie decreased over the next few days. This was an important success for Kalie, and this intervention provided behavioral data that Ms. Haygood could share with Kalie's foster parents to show that her instruction was having a positive impact on Kalie's behavior.

While each author of this book has been a teacher and is very cognizant of the time constraints of teachers, we still are very strong advocates of teachers doing simple interventions such as this that include simple, discrete counts of specific behavioral outbursts in the classroom. Only data such as these will show parents, foster parents, counselors, principals, other teachers, and the students themselves that progress is being made in curbing behavioral problems that can stem from trauma. In fact, sharing successful intervention results with children is strongly recommended, as this shows those children that they can learn to control their own behavior. In short, intervention data such as these are critical in dealing with these children, so we urge teachers to implement various interventions and then use these data to show the progress of students exposed to trauma. Many more case study examples are presented in this book.

SUMMARY

Becoming a trauma-informed school is step one in meeting the needs of kids exposed to trauma. As shown in the previous chapter, children and adolescents exposed to trauma will have varied and unique needs that simply cannot be met in traditional classrooms because traumatized brains are, literally, wired differently. To make any inroads with these deeply injured kids, schools simply have to do more, and faculty must strive to become trauma informed and implement appropriate teaching ideas and individual interventions. Although many techniques may be used that are effective with these students, this chapter has presented only a brief overview of the ideas that can be utilized. Later chapters in this book will focus on additional teaching tips and strategies for teachers to implement in their efforts to adequately meet the needs of these kids exposed to trauma.

REFERENCES

Adams, J. M. (2014, February 3). New "trauma-informed" approach to behavioral disorders in special education. *EdSource*. Retrieved from https://edsource.org/2014/new-trauma-informed-approach-to-behavioral-disorders-in-special-education/56753

Bender, W. N. (2012). *Differentiating instruction for students with learning disabilities: New best practices for general and special educators*. Corwin.

Centers for Disease Control and Prevention. (2021, April 6). *About the CDC-Kaiser ACE study*. Retrieved from https://www.cdc.gov/violenceprevention/aces/about.html

Chemtob, C. M., Novaco, R. W., Hamada, R. S., Gross, D. M., & Smith, G. (1997). Anger regulation deficits in combat-related posttraumatic stress disorder. *Journal of Traumatic Stress, 10*(1), 17–35.

Cole, S. F., Greenwald O'Brien, J., Geron Gadd, M., Ristuccia, J., Wallace, D. L., & Gregory, M. (2005). *Helping traumatized children learn: Supportive school environments for children traumatized by family violence*. A report and policy agenda. Massachusetts Advocates for Children: Trauma and Policy Initiative. Retrieved from https://traumasensitiveschools.org/wp-content/uploads/2013/06/Helping-Traumatized-Children-Learn.pdf

Craig, S. (2017). *Trauma-informed schools: Specific classroom strategies* [Audio interview]. Educator Summit 2017. Retrieved from https://www.attachmenttraumanetwork.org/atn-store-educator-2017-summit/

Doidge, N. (2007). *The brain that changes itself*. New York, NY: Penguin Books.

Eller, J. F., & Hierck, T. (2021). *Trauma-sensitive instruction: Creating a safe and predictable classroom environment*. Solution Tree.

Felitti, V., & Anda, R. (2009). *The adverse childhood experiences (ACE) study: Bridging the gap between childhood traumas and negative consequences later in life*. Retrieved from www.acestudy.org

Lebow, H. I. (2021, July 2). *The science behind PTSD symptoms: How trauma changes the brain*. PsychCentral. Retrieved from https://psychcentral.com/blog/the-science-behind-ptsd-symptoms-how-trauma-changes-the-brain/

Lippman, L., & Schmitz, H. (2013, October 30). *What can schools do to build resilience in their students?* Child Trends. Retrieved from https://childtrends.org/what-can-schools-do-to-build-resilience-in-their-students

Osofsky, J. D. (2019, December 18). *The effects of stress and trauma on language development*. Retrieved from https://www.speechpathology.com/articles/effects-stress-and-trauma-on-20323

Perry, B. D. (2000). Traumatized children: How childhood trauma influences brain development. *Journal of the California Alliance for the Mentally Ill, 11*(1), 48–51.

Perry, B. D. (2014). *Helping traumatized children: A brief overview for caregivers.* ChildTrauma Academy. Retrieved from https://www.childtr auma.org/_files/ugd/aa51c7_237459a7e16b4b7e9d2c4837c908eefe.pdf

Quirk, M. (2023, February 9). The benefits of mindfulness education in schools. *Psychology Today.* Retrieved from https://www.psychologytoday.com/us/ blog/evidence-based-living/202302/the-benefits-of-mindfulness-education-in-schools

Reinberg, S. (2021, August 10). *Pandemic has depression and anxiety rising globally among young people, data shows.* United Press International. Retrieved from https://www.upi.com/Health_News/2021/08/10/Pandemic-has-depression-anxiety-rising-globally-among-young-people-data-shows/ 1411628541635/

Rosenthal, M. (2021). Intergenerational Trauma: An Embodied Experience. *International Body Psychotherapy Journal. 20*(2), 80–86.

Simmons-Duffin, S. (2018, May 23). To teach kids to handle tough emotions, some schools take time out for group therapy. In *All things considered.* NPR. Retrieved from https://www.npr.org/sections/health-shots/2018/05/23/613 465023/for-troubled-kids-some-schools-take-time-out-for-group-therapy

Sousa, D. A. (2009). *How the brain influences behavior: Management strategies for every classroom.* Corwin.

Steffen, P. R., Hedges, D., & Matheson, R. (2022). The brain is adaptive not triune: How the brain responds to threat, challenge, and change. *Frontiers in Psychiatry, 13.* Retrieved from https://www.frontiersin.org/articles/10.33 89/fpsyt.2022.802606/full

CHAPTER 3

DEFUSING EXPLOSIVE BEHAVIORAL OUTBURSTS

TRIGGERS AND BEHAVIORAL EXPLOSIONS
Trauma and Lizard Brains in the Classroom

As discussed in Chapter 2, the brains of children repeatedly exposed to trauma are often hardwired for aggressive behavioral explosions because traumatizing home environments sometimes become the growth bed for aggression or violence (Perry, 2000, 2014). In their brains, the neural connections made in response to repeated, early trauma often ensure that their verbal and physical aggression is the *correct* response any time they perceive any type of threat in their environment. Such violence in response to being hit may have prevented them from being hit again in their home. Thus, these children might perceive virtually anything as a threat, which then elicits a verbally violent or physically violent response. Their violent responses often seem overreactive and out of place in the classroom, but for these children, virtually anything can trigger such a violent explosion (Craig, 2017; Perry, 2000) because of the hardwired neuronal connections in their brains resulting from trauma early in life.

In their minds, a threat might be any ordinary event in the classroom—something like having another student accidently brush their shoulder when they walk by, having someone stand too close, or having the teacher call on them for an answer that they may not know. All such stimuli may be interpreted as "aggression" in their minds, and as a result, it may seem that these kids "explode at everything!" These students often seem like ticking time bombs of rage or verbal aggression (Bender, 2016; Perry, 2014), and defusing these students early before a behavioral problem escalates is critical.

When such an emotional or aggressive outburst occurs, the teacher has landed right in the middle of a power struggle with the child exposed to repeated trauma. Moreover, when power struggles between teachers and students occur in the classroom, the student often wins (Albert, 1996; Bender, 2016). At that point, when a student's emotions are charged by surging "lizard brain" neurotransmitters in the brain, the student can and will invest everything in the power struggle. In contrast, the teacher cannot do so; the teacher is limited both by professional ethics and by the responsibility for other children in the class.

Please understand that we are not talking about mild behavioral infractions or disagreements in the classroom. Rather, we are talking about serious aggressive behavior, often explosive behaviors, and potentially dangerous emotionally charged situations. In such situations, the student exposed to trauma is fully invested in challenging the teacher's authority, defying instructions, and even cursing and hurling insults (or objects) at the teacher or others. Should such a student challenge a teacher in class in a verbally violent, enraged way, that student is emotionally dysregulated and probably believes they are protecting themselves. At that point, the "fight, flight, or freeze" (lizard brain) neural connections that developed in early childhood have become activated. In short, the lizard brain has taken over, and a self-protective survival instinct often using violence is governing the student's actions (Lebow, 2021). The student will say and do anything to "win" that power struggle.

Of course, teachers have the ultimate responsibility for maintaining discipline in the classroom, and while their options are limited in this situation, they can use an array of strategies to restore order. Traditional strategies included sending a student out of the room, or to the principal's office, or perhaps calling the school resource officer to remove an unsafe child from class. In those situations, professionals have to reflect: "Who won that power struggle? Didn't the student win by avoiding the learning activity completely?"

Further, engaging in a power struggle with an enraged student can be dangerous for both the out-of-control student and the teacher. Ron Walker (1998) indicated that in 75% of cases in which students physically attack teachers, there is some prelude or escalation period during the power struggle. This means that 75% of the time when teachers are physically attacked, they "saw it coming" and, thus, had some opportunity to avoid it! Avoiding those power plays with students, particularly students who have been repeatedly traumatized, is therefore not only effective from a disciplinary standpoint; it is also the safe choice for teachers.

Thus, one fundamental guideline is simple: When teaching kids exposed to trauma, avoid triggering power struggles with these students at all costs (Colvin, Ainge, & Nelson, 1997; Fast, 2019; Walker, 1998). Preventing the escalation of a power play with a misbehaving student is like defusing a ticking time bomb, and teachers are well advised to avoid, if at all possible, the explosion of anger or violence that they often see coming. Among veteran teachers, this skill is well developed, and they can usually avoid the power struggle in such a way as to allow the student some space and maybe even foster the development of a more positive relationship with the student. Numerous authors have indicated over the years that the most effective thing a teacher can do is choose to avoid the triggers for power plays as well as any student-created challenges to authority (Bender, 2016; Fast, 2019; Walker & Sylwester, 1998). Techniques for each are described as follows.

What Are Triggers?

A "trigger" is any situation or event that consistently initiates an explosive behavioral outburst in children (Bipolar Caregivers, n.d.; Fast, 2019; Frank, Gonzalez, & Fagioloni, 2006). For example, a teacher may ask a child to answer a question, and if the student doesn't know the answer, they may respond with a behavioral outburst (e.g., "I don't want to answer, and you can't make me!"). In other cases, one child standing near another or touching another may trigger a behavioral problem, and while all students, on occasion, are triggered into misbehavior, this phenomenon is particularly frequent among children with mood disorders, children with oppositional defiant disorder, and children exposed to repeated trauma.

In fact, for many of these students, numerous stimuli can be a trigger. Given that reality, presentation of any list of potential triggers may seem meaningless initially. Still, a general understanding of the types of events, transitions, or changes that might become triggers can be helpful. Box 3.1, compiled from a variety of sources, presents a list of potential triggers, some of which are controlled by the teacher and can often be avoided with judicious preparation (Bipolar Caregivers, n.d.; Fast, 2019; Frank et al., 2006).

Box 3.1 Potential triggers for students challenged by trauma

- *Stressful negative life events* (e.g., the birth of a sibling, marital problems between parents, ending a relationship with one parent or another, moving to a new house).

(Continued)

(Continued)

- *Disruption to sleep patterns* (e.g., due to neglect or lack of parental supervision). Decreases in the time a person sleeps can contribute to manic symptoms and/or depression.
- *Disruption to sleep routines.* A regular structure (e.g., regular children's bedtimes, regular waking-up times, regular evening activities) can help to maintain sleep patterns and energy levels.
- *Too much stimulation from external sources* (e.g., excessive classroom noise, clutter on a student's desk, traffic noises outside the school or on the playground, harsh lighting, crowded hallways).
- *Too much stimulation from within* (e.g., overstimulation from lots of activity, excitement about something at school).
- *Overuse of stimulating substances* like caffeine (e.g., in coffee or cola) or nicotine (e.g., in cigarettes or nicotine patches).
- *Abuse of alcohol or illegal drugs*, which can cause the user to have ongoing behavioral outbursts.
- *Conflict and stressful interactions* with teachers or classmates.
- *Disturbing or disruptive media or social media items*, particularly negative personal messages or news about stressful world events.
- *Abrupt transitions* between subjects, or disruptions during the school day.

Teachers should consider triggers on a child-by-child basis. Over time, teachers will understand that certain types of events are likely to trigger outbursts from specific students, and at that point, teachers may wish to develop their own list of triggers specifically for the children exposed to trauma and/or others in the class. Once such a list is developed, the teacher may wish to share that list with each child's parent or caregiver and ask if there are other things the parent has noticed that trigger the child. With the list thus completed, the teacher may be able to plan lessons to avoid those child-specific triggers.

BEST TEACHING PRACTICES

In addition to specific triggers for particular children, some routine events in school, such as transitions between subjects, unexpected tests, and so forth, seem to trigger many students' misbehaviors. Although some of these are necessary in the process of teaching, others can often be avoided (Hall, Williams, & Hall, 2000; McIntosh, Herman, Stanford, McGraw, & Florence, 2004).

Emphasize Consistency

Embedded within the desire for control of their environment among children exposed to trauma is a need for consistency in the classroom. It is quite difficult, if not impossible, to sense that one has any personal control if the classroom environment is not consistent. Thus, for students exposed to trauma—and, in fact, for most children—a consistent classroom environment is paramount. Teachers should generally maintain consistent rules for classroom behavior, consistency in order of the daily activities, and absolute consistency in their relationships with the students. Students exposed to multiple adverse childhood experiences (ACEs) will only engage in more social interaction with a teacher or counselor when they sense the safety that a consistent environment brings.

Use Warnings Before Transitions

Preparing students for class transitions is also critical. Simply letting students know that a transition of some type is coming can help reduce some behavioral problems (Bender, 2016), so teachers should get into the habit of warning kids about coming transitions. Warning students who are overly sensitive to change about coming transitions helps them mentally prepare for the transition, and they are less likely to feel frustration. In preparing for a coming transition, a teacher might warn the class using a statement such as "We'll be starting our math in about five minutes, once we are finished writing our paragraphs. Sometimes you guys get too loud when we change subjects, so for the next three minutes, everything in class has to be said in a whisper! This will help us avoid any problems as a team."

Use Peer Buddies

We suggest that teachers use a peer buddy system that partners students together for some transitions as well as some of their work assignments. In many cases, a partner of a student with behavioral issues will assist in curbing misbehavior. Once peer buddies are identified for everyone in the class, teachers might say something like "Okay. Put away your math books and get out your history books. Once your history book is out, and you are ready, remember to check with your peer buddy, and help them get ready, if they need it. In this class, we like to help each other."

However, teachers and clinicians should be aware that this is not a strategy to use for all students exposed to trauma. Excessively shy or withdrawn children will not or cannot work well with peer buddies without extensive preparation and coaching. Still, teachers should consider this option for most students challenged by repeated trauma.

Teach Appropriate Behaviors for Transitions

In addition to warnings of transitions, teachers should specifically teach how to complete transitions. Many children exposed to trauma are very disorganized, and this, like many of their behaviors, may be rooted in dysfunctional neuronal connections in the brain (Perry, 2014). Many of these kids may appear disoriented when asked to simply form a line or complete other simple tasks, and some teachers may find themselves wondering how a student can manage to not understand such a simple request. Of course, such behavior may result from other things as well, such as social frustration or isolation. Highly disorganized kids, as well as socially isolated students, may be paralyzed during the "get in line" process, as they wonder, "Who should I stand next to?" They may end up far out of line, standing in the middle of the classroom, staring at the line rather than entering into it, while everyone else lines up nicely along the wall. To alleviate this problem, teachers should give specific instructions to these children. Here are a couple of examples.

- ▶ "Stacy, I'd like you to be our leader, so please come right to the front of the line and stand close to me. I might need you to help me out."
- ▶ "Jason, please get in line behind your peer buddy Treavor, and tomorrow it will be your turn to stand in front of Treavor."

Use a Calming Voice to Call Students by Name

Often, calling students by name, using a soft, easy tone of voice, will help calm them, and this is particularly recommended for students exposed to trauma (Craig, 2017). For example, the teacher might say, "Anthony, I can see that you are working hard today, and I just want you to know that I appreciate that! I'm really glad to have you in my class!"

Further, even in intense disciplinary situations, teachers should make a conscious effort to use a calming voice. In fact, this calming technique is used by police forces worldwide to defuse angry perpetrators because it is so very effective. Again, this goes back to brain-related behaviors. The brains of all human beings are hardwired neurologically to match those we are talking to in a variety of areas including voice volume, voice tone, emotional intensity, physical stance, and even facial expressions (Bender, 2016). In some intense classroom situations—perhaps a noncompliant student shouting curses at a teacher—the teacher will have a natural inclination to match the voice tone, volume, and emotional intensity of the student, and that will only escalate the situation, sometimes resulting in an explosion of violence.

However, with some practice, teachers in these explosive student-created situations can use this hardwired brain-based behavior to de-escalate a potentially explosive student. Instead of adding to the escalation of an emotional, explosive situation, the teacher's use of a calming voice tone and volume can, in effect, "invite" the student to match the teacher on a calmer level without so much emotional intensity. This will take some practice on the part of the teacher, but it is well worth the effort when managing students exposed to repeated trauma.

Compliment Students Exposed to Trauma

Although teachers should always avoid false praise, they should make a habit of complimenting students exposed to trauma whenever they can. This will help establish trust and build a positive relationship, as well as helping to foster improved behavior. As one might imagine, children exposed to trauma have not experienced an overabundance of compliments in their lives, and this simple habit of giving deserved compliments can help these students feel valued in ways that they may not have experienced previously.

Stand Next to Students Exposed to Trauma

We suggest that, for each transition in class, teachers position themselves near their students exposed to trauma. At times, being within an arm's reach can alleviate any problem. Also, when unexpected events occur, teachers should physically move toward specific students with behavioral problems as quickly as possible, without moving in an aggressive manner, but in such a way as to help redirect the child toward more appropriate behavior.

Offer Choices

This teaching tip cannot be overemphasized. Offering choices can empower students who, because of their background, have an ingrained need to retain some control over their surroundings. Offering choices may, in fact, prevent class disruption. Teachers, for example, frequently develop various versions of the same general assignment in order to differentiate the work for students in the class who may need more of a challenge. Imagine an advanced yet overly shy student who is being raised in a foster home because of some trauma in his family situation. To provide that student a choice, the teacher might say, "Jamie, I usually give you a few more problems than some of the other students because you are really, really fast, but today I'll give you a choice. If you promise that you'll work hard and be willing to help other students after you finish, I'll let you choose to do fewer problems and complete those on the computer. Are you willing to do that, and if so, how many problems do you think you should do before helping others?"

Give Singular, Precise Instructions

Providing precise instructions, one at a time, is one example of consistency in the classroom. Children exposed to trauma function best when there is little ambiguity in their world. Thus, teachers should get in the habit of giving clear, short, directive commands and using pauses to break up multiple instructions. Rather than stringing three or four different transition tasks together, teachers might say, "Okay, please put away your math worksheet." The teacher could then wait four or five seconds, giving students time to complete that task, before saying, "Get out your social studies book." Then, after another pause, the teacher might say, "Turn to page 265." These short, specific instructions help disorganized kids complete the class transitions much more smoothly, and with less frustration, than in situations in which the teacher issues all those commands together.

Establish Clear Class Routines

Knowing what comes next is essential for almost all students, and in particular for students exposed to trauma. In the elementary grades, posting a daily schedule on a smartboard or the wall can help with transitions and perhaps alleviate some class disruption. The schedule should include, at a minimum, what subjects teachers will teach and when, and when class breaks occur. Because consistency and predictability are crucial for kids exposed to trauma, the teacher should refer to that schedule often and stick to it each day, if at all possible. Of course, changes in class routine are sometimes necessary and often enrich the class, but they also may be a trigger for students exposed to trauma (Bender, 2016).

AVOIDING POWER PLAYS WITH DEFUSING TECHNIQUES

In addition to avoiding triggers, teachers must learn to extract themselves from power plays that children exposed to trauma will sometimes create. Should a student, for seemingly no reason, burst into cursing in the class, that student is essentially daring the teacher to take some disciplinary action. Thus, a power play has been set up, and it is not inaccurate to say that the student, at that moment, is daring the teacher to do something, which will then set off a behavioral explosion!

Unfortunately, that is a situation teachers often find themselves in with kids exposed to trauma. These students sometimes set up challenges to teacher authority as a means to establish more control over their environment, or they may merely wish to avoid whatever subject or assignment they believed was coming next in the class.

In these power struggles, the usual disciplinary contingencies and interventions are not particularly useful (Craig, 2017). Sending the child out of class or using other typical punishments does not work well with students exposed to repeated trauma. Rather, in power play situations, teachers should seek to escape the power play without triggering the student into a behavioral outburst by using one or more of the common defusing techniques presented here. These have the advantage of extracting both the teacher and the student from the power play, and hopefully avoiding the trigger that might send the student into full behavioral meltdown. Also, managing such situations wisely may even help the teacher build a more positive relationship with the student over time. Once teachers avoid the immediate power play, they can deal with the disruption a bit later by talking with the student after class, or by planning a longer-term behavioral intervention should one be necessary.

We suggest that all teachers become comfortable with several of these defusing techniques, and if the first attempt to calm the student doesn't work, teachers should try another! Teachers should be prepared, on a moment's notice, to use these defusing techniques. These ideas come from a variety of sources (Albert, 1996; Colvin et al., 1997; Walker & Sylwester, 1998) and generally allow the teacher to escape power struggles with students and help regulate the situation.

Inquire About a Student's Anger

If a student looks angry or upset and time allows, the teacher should ask about that anger (Bender, 2016). The teacher might say something like "I can see that the assignment upsets you. Is it something we need to talk about?" Clearly, teachers would rather take a moment and have a brief discussion about the student's concern than have to deal with an anger explosion or other power play in class. Teachers should, however, be cautious with this tactic because it might lead to a lengthy discussion with the student, and class time is always at a premium.

Respect Students' Personal Space

Personal space is the physical space surrounding someone, and all teachers should understand how to use personal space when dealing with kids exposed to trauma, and other explosive children. In the United States and most Westernized countries, personal space extends in an oval shape, about two and a half feet in front of the body but only six inches or so to the side and rear. Almost all U.S. citizens become quite uncomfortable if another person enters that personal space; we might even feel as if the other person is "invading" our space. In short, someone entering our personal space is an aggressive move on their part, and most of us interpret it as such. There are differences in various cultures (e.g., personal space is viewed quite differently in certain Middle Eastern and Asian cultures), but in general, getting into the personal space of schoolchildren is not recommended. This is particularly true for students exposed to repeated trauma.

Because of the threat of aggression associated with invasion of personal space, such an invasion can trigger responsive aggression among kids exposed to trauma. In fact, many kids exposed to trauma are victims of abuse, rape, and so on, which clearly is the extreme violation of personal space. Thus, the wiring in the brains of kids exposed to trauma makes aggression a go-to response for invasions of personal space (Perry, 2014). For these kids, such a personal space invasion will frequently trigger an attack.

Almost all police officers have some training in the use of personal space when apprehending perpetrators and/or other angry individuals. This training empowers them to manage explosive anger in most situations. However, teachers only rarely receive such training, so use of personal space is not something teachers routinely do. Still, teachers who wish to succeed with students exposed to trauma should learn to stay out of the personal space of students at all times, unless the student is attempting to self-harm or harm others. Like most teachers before entering the classroom, the authors of this book were not taught to use personal space in disciplinary situations, and that led to a major problem in one particular situation early in Dr. Bender's teaching career.

Vignette 3.1 Dr. Bender's bad decisions

In managing the misbehavior of a student—Joanne—during my first year of teaching, I invaded her personal space. Joanne was being raised by her grandmother because of parental drug addiction in her former home. There had been allegations of child neglect also, though not of any physical abuse. Still, I considered none of that when she challenged my authority! Seemingly out of nowhere one day, she shouted that she would not complete an assignment, and then she cursed at me. Next, she slammed her book down on the desk, and then put her head down.

I felt that my disciplinary authority had been challenged, so I responded. As I did so, I turned to her, surprised by the outburst, and then marched directly toward her across the classroom. That was an aggressive move—mistake number one.

I shouted back at her as I self-righteously trod along (mistake number two)! Without thinking about it, I had matched her voice volume, voice tone, and emotional intensity! "Oh, yes, you will, Joanne!" I shouted. "Now get that book open and get started!" By the time I'd finished that sentence, I found myself hovering over the front of her desk, and by that point, she was rising to the challenge, getting up, and about to come across that desk at me!

I realized I was about to be physically attacked. I saw vicious anger and, I realized later, great pain on her face. It was only then that I backed away a few steps. She then stopped, still looking at me and ready to kill. Clearly, I had marched, most stupidly, right into her personal space! That was mistake number three!

How very foolish I was in my first year of teaching! One need only reflect that after her verbal outburst, Joanne had already put her head on her desk. Why did I not just leave it there for a couple minutes?

Again, most teachers are not taught about students' personal space, but they should be because such insight can frequently prevent the escalation of violence when dealing with many violent students, as well as students exposed to trauma. Clearly,

(Continued)

Vignette 3.1 (Continued)

these moves on my part—matching Joanne's emotional energy and decibel level, and moving toward her and thus invading her personal space—exacerbated a bad situation. My only excuse is that I was, then, a brand-new teacher, and I knew nothing about personal space, and even less about management of students living in crisis.

Today, as a veteran teacher knowing much more about these matters, I would do the exact opposite. Rather than move toward her, I would merely have looked directly at her, which would have been a much less aggressive move on my part. Next, I would have sidetracked the power play escalation by responding in a much softer voice, perhaps by asking her a question about her anger. I might say something like "Joanne, I can see you are upset, and I'm sorry if I've done something that upset you. Can you help me understand why you're angry?"

In short, had I been taught to use personal space awareness and voice tone in my disciplinary practices, I am confident I would have managed that situation much, much better. As it turned out, Joanne was angry with something said to her before she even entered my class, and I was merely unlucky enough to catch her pain and anger! Still, today, I believe I could have defused that explosion. Again, knowing these simple techniques—avoiding triggers, using voice tone and volume, avoiding entering personal space—will help all teachers manage kids exposed to trauma much more effectively.

And one more bit of honesty here: Hasn't every veteran teacher reflected on how little we really knew during our first year of teaching? We should all be more forgiving of ourselves for that, but let's also find in that reality a determined motivation to manage these students more effectively.

Repeat the Instructions

When a teacher gives instructions and a student challenges them or disrupts class in some other way, one option is to softly but firmly repeat the instruction rather than respond directly to the student's challenge. It is very hard to argue with someone who is not addressing the challenged point directly but rather is merely saying the same thing repeatedly. After two or three repetitions, students might stop making counterarguments since the teacher is not responding to those anyway. They then will generally, often reluctantly, begin their work.

Teachers should therefore repeat the instructions, word for word if possible, in a calm voice two or three times after each challenge. This repetition of instructions, like all disciplinary techniques, will not work all the time, but it will work frequently.

Here is an example: A teacher gives the directions, "Please put your English book away and take out your history text." One student then shouts, "I don't want to do history today!" This verbal challenge holds the potential of becoming a transition disruption in the class, so the teacher responds by moving toward that student a few steps (while avoiding personal space) and softly repeating the instructions: "I said, please put your English book away and take out your history text." By using a softer voice tone and volume than the student, the teacher is encouraging the student to match that softer voice tone. Most of the time, students will persist with yet another verbal challenge, such as "Do we have to? History is so boring!" Again, the teacher should softly repeat the instructions: "I said, please put your English book away and take out your history text."

This idea often works for one simple reason. It is difficult to argue with someone who is merely repeating themselves. After three or four such gently spoken repetitions, the student will, in many cases, desist in the challenge. At that point, the teacher should walk away and begin to assist another student. This will sometimes allow the offending student to calm down a bit. However, teachers should never turn their back on a student who has challenged them. Also, if a behavioral explosion occurs anyway, the teacher will need to use another, stronger defusing idea.

Make a Joke

Well-timed humor that is not directed in any way at the student can often defuse a student's anger (Albert, 1996). In the situation described in Vignette 3.1, Dr. Bender could have merely backed away and replied, "Well, that's one way to go." That humor, if directed at anyone, would have been directed at that teacher's own ability to control the classroom and not at the student's cursing. Still, such a joke may have allowed an escape from an overt power play with Joanne. Of course, this recommendation to use humor should never involve a joke about the student or at the student's expense. Still, a bit of humor, unrelated to the specific noncompliance, can sometimes defuse a behavioral outburst before it happens.

Share Power

We also recommend that teachers be prepared to share power in the classroom, up to a limit, with students. If a student challenges the teacher on an assignment or task and mentions something else they would like to do, the teacher should be in a position, at least some of the time, to negotiate with the student and therefore share power concerning when the student may do the tasks (Colvin et al., 1997). In this instance, the teacher might say something like "Okay, Tyrone has suggested that we do something more fun than this math worksheet, so maybe we can do a math game today. We'll do that today, if you guys agree that we'll do this math worksheet tomorrow! Does everyone agree?"

Even this small acknowledgment of the student's power can often improve class climate and might avoid conflict for some kids. Again, control over one's environment is critical for children exposed to trauma, and some power sharing is crucial for a trauma-informed classroom.

Postpone the Disciplinary Discussion

Finally, postponing discussion of a student's misbehavior is often an appropriate tactic (Albert, 1996). After a disciplinary issue arises, it is typically advisable to talk with the student, but sometimes postponing that "disciplinary debrief" until the student is calmer is wise. If a student is highly emotionally charged, the teacher might let the student know that they want to discuss the problem at a later time, perhaps at the end of the period. Sometimes, merely knowing that a caring adult is interested can defuse a student's anger or rage, and sometimes allows the student time to calm down a bit.

A CASE STUDY: REPEATED INSTRUCTIONS

Many of the teaching ideas in this chapter involve establishing good teaching habits, but others can be used as targeted interventions. Here is a case study example. In his sixth-grade mathematics class, Mr. Johnson found himself in repeated power struggles with Janice. Janice often refused to complete work in class, and at other times, she was not turning in any homework.

For example, Mr. Johnson said, "I want you folks to do the three rows of problems at the top of page 289 for homework."

Before he even completed the sentence, Janice said, "We shouldn't have any homework tonight. We have a home football game this afternoon!"

Of course, on the face of it, that statement sounds reasonable, at least from a student's perspective. Mr. Johnson, without thinking, responded directly to the issue raised: "Okay, guys, get real! Most of you don't even go to the football games." Being a veteran teacher, he knew he had made a mistake as soon as he said it. In effect, he had responded to a student's objection to the assignment instead of merely repeating the assignment. Thus, in effect, he had invited everyone else in the class to protest that they were indeed going to the football game later that day! Within a few seconds, no fewer than five other students were stating loudly that they were definitely going to the game, and therefore should have no homework!

Later that afternoon, Mr. Johnson reflected on the matter, and he realized that he had fallen into Janice's power play trap. He'd participated in a power struggle. Further, he realized that, all too often, he had responded to a student's point in such situations when, in reality, the student was not trying to make a reasonable request but merely trying to avoid work. Mr. Johnson decided he needed to break his habit of responding directly to such student comments, and he determined to change his behavior, and Janice's behavior as well.

For the next three days, Mr. Johnson noted the number of times that Janice objected to class work or homework or disrupted the class with any type of power struggle. He then put that baseline data on a chart, as presented in Figure 3.1. As the data show, Janice was initiating a power struggle between three and four times each day.

Mr. Johnson chose to use a "repeated instruction" tactic as the intervention for Janice. When she protested an assignment or began any other misbehavior, he would merely repeat the instructions. He began that intervention on the next day and continued it for two weeks, while carefully counting the power struggle challenges from Janice. Each time Janice initiated a disciplinary challenge, Mr. Johnson used a softer voice and repeated the instructions. If she challenged him again, he merely repeated the instructions a second, or even a third, time.

As the intervention data show, Janice responded fairly quickly to this intervention. It is a fact that few students will continue an argument when the teacher is using a soft voice and merely saying the same thing repeatedly. In this instance, the data show that within five days, the number of power struggle challenges began to decrease. By the end of the second week, Mr. Johnson's repeated instructions intervention had all but eliminated Janice's attempts to initiate a power struggle.

Figure 3.1 • *Janice's class disruptions intervention*

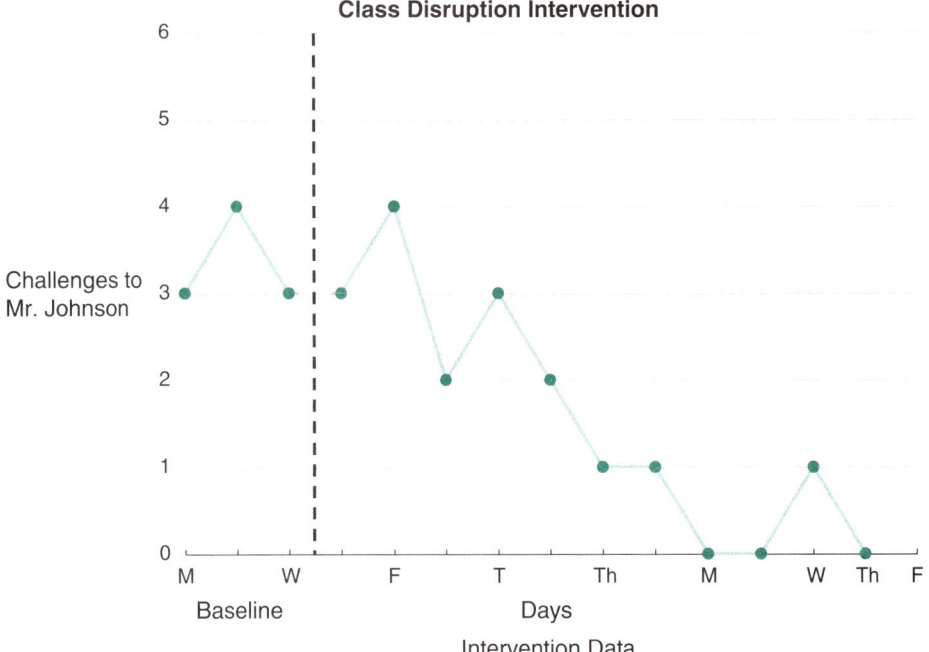

As one interesting side effect of this intervention, Mr. Johnson noticed that other students also had reduced their verbal challenges to his assignments. He had not kept any data on other students' challenges of assignments, but he did notice an improvement in overall class climate because of this simple intervention. In that sense, not only had Mr. Johnson curbed a potential problem with Janice, but he had indirectly improved behavior of several other students as well.

SUMMARY

Avoiding triggers is critical for teachers working with students exposed to trauma, and it is strongly recommended not only for these kids but for all students. Knowing what may trigger a behavioral problem and finding creative ways to avoid that trigger can prevent a behavioral outburst and is essential in trauma-informed schools. In fact, it is the only way to begin to reach and teach these kids exposed to trauma.

Likewise, avoiding power plays initiated by these students is critical, as most veteran teachers realize. Many students who are repeatedly exposed to trauma seem to be masters of creating power struggles with teachers, because that singular skill may have helped them achieve more control at home, or perhaps even survive amid a chaotic home life. Of course, teachers simply have too many responsibilities to waste time in power struggles that can be avoided, so knowing and employing these techniques to avoid them should be considered "basic survival skills" by teachers and clinicians who serve children exposed to trauma.

REFERENCES

Albert, L. (1996). *Cooperative Discipline*. Circle Pines, MN: American Guidance Service.

Bender, W. N. (2016). *20 Disciplinary Strategies for working with Challenging Students*. FL: Learning Sciences International.

Bipolar Caregivers. (n.d.). *Common bipolar triggers*. Retrieved from https://bipolarcaregivers.org/treatment-and-management/common-bipolar-triggers

Colvin, G., Ainge, D., & Nelson, R. (1997). How to defuse confrontations. *Exceptional Children*, *64*, 47–51.

Craig, S. (2017). *Trauma-informed schools: Specific classroom strategies* [Audio interview]. Educator Summit 2017. Retrieved from https://www.attach menttraumanetwork.org/atn-store-educator-2017-summit/

Fast, J. (2019, June 2). What are triggers and how do they affect bipolar disorder? HealthyPlace. Retrieved from https://www.healthyplace.com/bipolar-disorder/bipolar-treatment/how-triggers-affect-bipolar-disorder-gsd

Frank, E., Gonzalez, J. M., & Fagioloni, A. (2006). The importance of routine for preventing recurrence in bipolar disorder. *American Journal of Psychiatry*, *163*(6), 981–985.

Hall, N., Williams, J., & Hall, P. D. (2000). Fresh approaches with oppositional students. *Reclaiming Children and Youth*, *8*, 291.

Lebow, H. I. (2021, July 2). *The science behind PTSD symptoms: How trauma changes the brain*. PsychCentral. Retrieved from https://psychcentral.com/blog/the-science-behind-ptsd-symptoms-how-trauma-changes-the-brain/

McIntosh, K., Herman, K., Stanford, A., McGraw, K., & Florence, K. (2004). Teaching transition: Techniques for promoting success between lessons. *Teaching Exceptional Children*, *37*, 26–31.

Perry, B. D. (2000). Children exposed to trauma: How childhood trauma influences brain development. *Journal of the California Alliance for the Mentally Ill, 11*(1), 48–51.

Perry, B. D. (2014). *Helping children exposed to trauma: A brief overview for caregivers.* ChildTrauma Academy. Retrieved from https://www.childtrauma.org/_files/ugd/aa51c7_237459a7e16b4b7e9d2c4837c908eefe.pdf

Walker, R. (1998). Discipline without disruption [Presentation]. In W. N. Bender & P. McLaughlin (Eds.), *Tough kid professional development teleconference.* Athens, GA: University of Georgia.

Walker, H., & Sylwester, B. (1998). Reducing students' refusal and resistance. *Teaching Exceptional Children, 30*(6), 52–58.

CHAPTER 4

SENSORY SUPPORT IN THE CLASSROOM

SENSORY INPUT AND TRAUMA

Many sources have documented the fact that children exposed to trauma frequently experience difficulties interpreting data from their own senses, or even distortions in sensory integration (Perry, 2000, 2014; Robinson & Brown, 2016; van der Kolk, 2014). Sensory integration is a neurobiological process involving the organization of stimuli from the environment with sensations from an individual's body in order to make sense of and interact effectively with the surrounding environment. When an individual experiences an atypical response to sensory input, it can be difficult to navigate everyday experiences and responsibilities. A child experiencing disorganized sensory input may feel overwhelmed by auditory, tactile, or visual input (Schaff et al., 2010). Further, while children are experiencing disorganized sensory input, it becomes difficult to simultaneously manage emotions and behaviors. The resulting dysregulated emotions and behaviors may include distractibility, impulsiveness, aggression, or anxiety (Joseph, Casteleijn, van der Linde, & Franzsen, 2021).

While many children experience sensory processing disorders without having experienced trauma, research shows that sensory processing issues are clinically significant in students who have suffered abuse or other trauma (Morin, 2023; Perry, 2014; Robinson & Brown, 2016). The general impact of trauma on children's brains was presented in Chapter 2, but teachers and clinicians must understand and address several specific issues, such as memory processing and dysregulation, resulting from sensory integration issues based on trauma experienced in childhood. It is not an overstatement to say that understanding the lizard brain's threat-seeking self-preservation techniques is crucial for teachers in serving students exposed to trauma. Not only does this understanding tend to foster use of evidence-based practices, but such understanding also creates a sense of empathy when addressing these students in general.

Trauma and Memory

Children who have experienced trauma show different levels of activity in several brain regions involved with memory and memory processing (Perry, 2014; van der Kolk, 2014). Both the amygdala (which interprets sensory data and processes reptilian brain threat-seeking processes) and the hippocampus (associated with recognition memory) are impacted by early trauma, so children exposed to trauma will process memories in ways that are different from other children. Children who are repeatedly exposed to trauma are likely to have both explicit and implicit memories of specific traumatic events. While explicit memories are conscious and can often be dealt with via verbal discussions in therapy, implicit memories are automatic and are not verbally articulated easily. Thus, these memories are more difficult to address.

When a child experiences trauma, sensory awareness is heightened in a protective manner, and this leaves traumatic memories stored in disjointed, or fragmented, pieces of sensory information. These memories are often encoded in a disorganized manner and may include information about the environment where the trauma took place, physical sensations, emotional reactions at the time of the trauma, and sensory input received at the time of the traumatic event. Implicit memories may include almost any stimuli such as the smell of an abuser's perfume, the color of the walls in the room where a trauma took place, or noises that are related to the crisis experienced. When these implicit memories are triggered in future situations or other similar environments, children exposed to trauma may react with dysregulated and frequently uncontrolled emotions or behaviors, which in their minds function as a means of self-preservation.

Trauma and Dysregulation

As described in Chapter 2, once a student's amygdala signals to the brain that there is perceived danger (whether that danger is real or perceived does not matter to the lizard brain), many systems are unconsciously activated in the body and central nervous system in order to protect the student. In addition to heightened threat-seeking in the amygdala, the prefrontal cortex in the child's brain essentially "shuts down," and the student is, for a time, neurologically incapable of accessing skills like rational thinking, problem solving, and creative thinking. Of course, these are the exact thought processes that help individuals regulate their emotions and behaviors. Thus, students exposed to trauma are, typically, much less able to "self-regulate" emotions, moods, and behaviors than are other students. This will be blatantly obvious in the classroom, where seemingly meaningless stimuli, embedded within nonspecific implicant memories, may trigger extreme emotions or inappropriate behaviors in students exposed to trauma.

In moments of such dysregulation, it is unrealistic and unfair to expect the student to be able to think rationally. Asking the student "Why is that upsetting you?" or "What do you think would help?" will not support the student in such situations, and could possibly cause further dysregulation. Until such students have developed better self-regulation skills, they will not be able to respond to these questions in a rational or helpful way. Thus, one can understand the need to teach these children to use their "smart part" brain well in advance.

In situations like this, teachers must also make certain that they are personally prepared, in an emotional sense, to support these students. The most critical aspect of supporting a dysregulated student is remaining regulated as the caregiver, because a dysregulated adult—an overly emotional, verbally loud, or even angry adult—will only signal more danger to the child. If teachers are unable to maintain a calm, caring manner, they should extract themselves from the situation as they can, and immediately seek support from another adult.

A SENSORY-SAFE CLASS ENVIRONMENT

Having noted these brain-based issues, it becomes clear how difficult it can be to serve children exposed to trauma in the classroom. In fact, it is virtually impossible to dictate a single, specific design for a sensory-safe environment for every student who has experienced trauma as each child's sensory triggers will vary, ranging from the lighting to unexpected sounds in the classroom. Some students exposed to trauma actually seek out more sensory experiences, and these sensory-seeking students may engage in behaviors that are considered disruptive such as pushing others, or using materials inappropriately, in order to increase their sensations.

Sensory avoiders, in contrast, may appear distracted and struggle with transitions, loud noises, and more chaotic classroom activities (Wild & Steeley, 2018). With the wide range of ways that students experience sensory stressors, having a variety of sensory options available in the classroom is the optimal approach to providing a sensory-safe environment.

Physical Space

Research has found that children and teens who have experienced trauma can be more sensitive to physical input. They may not find comfort in social supports such as physical touch, close proximity to teachers or others, or eye contact (Margolin & Vickerman, 2007). In contrast, other students exposed to trauma respond well to these very stimuli. When designing the classroom, teachers must recognize and respect these differing sensitivities by ensuring there is adequate space for movement and that students have choices for their own seating location. Some students may need to sit in the back of the class, somewhat away from others, while others may need to be near the teacher in front. Also, in the trauma-informed elementary classroom, a teacher may welcome students to the floor for morning meeting while allowing some students to choose a more removed space and flexible seating options (using a yoga ball away from the carpet area, sitting behind the general morning meeting area on a stool, etc.).

Visual Input

Educators should consider using lamps and softer lighting to avoid the bright fluorescent lights occasionally found in classrooms. Studies have shown that students appear more relaxed and engaged in classroom activities when brightness is reduced (Winterbottom & Wilkins, 2009). This research documented the impact of fluorescent lights, showing that their intensity can aggravate hyperactivity in children. We should note that various studies of classroom lighting are focused on all learners and do not specifically highlight the impact of increased sensitivity to sensory input due to trauma. Therefore, by reducing the brightness and flicker of lights in the classroom, educators are often able to support many sensory-sensitive students in a trauma-informed classroom.

Auditory Input

A trauma-informed classroom is a "noise limited" classroom. Teachers are becoming more aware of students' possible aversion to loud noises due to heightened stages of hypervigilance. When creating a class environment for students who have been exposed to trauma, teachers must consider having tools readily available for auditory aversion. Students may become dysregulated during fire drills, when a bell rings, or when the volume is naturally increased such as during physical education, during music classes, or in the cafeteria. Therefore, teachers should have options for students to use such as ear plugs or noise-reducing headphones during these times of the day. Of course, tools such as noise-reducing headphones are only effective if a student is aware of and able to request use of the tools.

To use these tools effectively, noise stressors must be made as predictable as possible. The students also need to be aware of the schedule (e.g., anticipated bell ringing at the end of an academic period), trust in the schedule's predictability, and have a plan for incidents that occur outside of the regular schedule. Research consistently shows that part of a trauma-informed approach is ensuring there is trustworthiness in the schedule and choice in dealing with anticipated and unanticipated noise stressors (Sweetman, 2022). By consistently following a schedule and classroom protocols that are firmly set in place, predictability, and ultimately trust, is established.

A School Safety Plan

Many if not most schools today have already developed school safety plans that are quite comprehensive as a result of issues such as concerns involving school security, intruders, or random shooting incidents. These plans are typically prepared ahead of time, and will include topics such as disaster-specific training (preparing for earthquakes, floods, gas leaks, etc.), bomb threats, campus security and lockdown procedures, and periodic fire drills. Some schools have moved further to include topics such as food allergy training or first aid training for selected staff, and such additions to the school safety plan are recommended. If such a plan is in place and includes the possibility of immediate calls for help and other topics that are particularly relevant to children exposed to trauma, then there is no need for any additional planning.

However, because of the dysregulation issues among students exposed to trauma, the trauma-informed school should include a variety of specific procedures for instances in which a child loses control. Such a plan might involve a list of "support persons" whom a teacher could summon immediately, when help is needed in the classroom, or a set of "code words" for teachers to use to communicate with other adults. For example, knowing that one might call on the teacher across the hall, a guidance counselor, or an administrator with a simple coded message delivered by another student—such as "code white," meaning "Get to my classroom immediately and help!"—will give teachers options should a student's dysregulated emotions or behaviors get out of hand. Box 4.1 presents this and several other ideas to be included in school safety plans, which are important for students exposed to trauma.

Box 4.1 Ideas for a trauma-informed safety plan

- **Adult code words:** Code words are kept secret, and might be used to signal an immediate call for help. Teachers might send a student to a principal's office, a counselor's office, or another classroom with instructions to use these particular code words once there.
- **"Help required" signals:** Other nonverbal signals that are kept secret, that a teacher can use, might be devised to indicate an immediate need for assistance (a ribbon thumbtacked to a door, specific hand signals teachers might show to other teachers on the playground, etc.).
- **Movement/evacuation plans:** Plans to evacuate a single classroom in an orderly fashion should be put in place, for use if a student loses control completely and becomes violent.
- **Nonclassroom safe spaces:** Schools should identify and teach students about nonclassroom safe spaces (e.g., a principal's office or counselor's office). When children are under stress and their emotions are completely dysregulated, such prior instruction on safe spaces in the school can be critical.
- **Abuse/neglect reporting procedures:** These procedures are required by law in most states, and such reporting procedures should be discussed yearly with faculty (particularly new faculty) and printed out for all adults in the school.
- **Bullying and cyberbullying policies:** With increasing attention to bullying and cyberbullying, more schools are including appropriate anti-bullying policies in school safety plans. Students should be taught how to respond to bullying and cyberbullying, and how to let a teacher or counselor know when they are being bullied.

A Calming Corner

Helping students establish improved self-regulation is critical for those exposed to trauma, and many ideas in this text will assist in that endeavor. One critical idea is providing a safe space or calming corner in the classroom to which children can retire to help themselves reestablish emotional equilibrium (Morin, 2023; Noddings, 2017). Children exposed to trauma are almost always stressed, because they are so highly reactive to sensory stimuli. Therefore, feeling safe and calm is a huge issue because many of these kids do not experience those feelings in their own homes (Craig, 2017). Therefore, when setting up a trauma-informed classroom, educators should have space for students to isolate when they feel it is necessary, and this is typically referred to as a "calming corner." This is simply a quiet place where students can feel safe and then independently use the strategies they are taught and the tools provided to regulate themselves.

The calming corner may be as simple as a rug, a comfortable rocking chair, or an inviting cushion on the floor in a back corner of the room. This "back corner" placement typically puts these children where they can see others in the class, but not be viewed by others, while still remaining within sight of the teacher. The calming corner allows students to escape from the class for two or three minutes (or more as necessary) at any time they choose.

While a calming corner is essential for students exposed to trauma, it is quite useful for many students with various behavior problems. Thus, all students in the class should be taught to retreat to the calming corner when they feel angry, frightened, or nervous. This will allow them to begin to de-escalate in an emotionally charged situation and will thus help these children develop a sense of control over their fears or other threatening emotions. Also, when a teacher sees a student in the calming corner, the teacher should make a point of allowing two or three minutes for the student to calm down and then walk over to say, "Let me know if I can help." This simple statement is preferable to any question (e.g., "Are you okay?" or "Can I help?") since questions may increase a child's confusion. Thus, a simple offer of help is best. The calming corner will probably help prevent behavioral outbursts by many students in the classroom, but for children exposed to trauma, having the choice of going to a safe space rather than acting out can be critical. Box 4.2 presents suggestions for creating a calming corner.

Box 4.2 Creating a calming corner

While calming corners have become more popular in elementary school classrooms, these spaces for support can be highly effective with older learners as well. A calming corner provides opportunity for choice; students are able to identify their own need for support and engage with strategies and tools that are specifically designed to help promote emotional regulation. Here are a few tips for getting started with a calming corner in any classroom.

(Continued)

(Continued)

- **Consider corner location:** Students seeking a calming corner are looking for isolation in order to regulate. While teachers need to be able to monitor student behavior, the more isolated individual learners feel from glances of peers and teachers, the faster they will be able to regulate their own behavior and emotions.

- **Create a comfortable corner:** For students who have experienced trauma, the brain is in a hypervigilant state and working to respond to potential signs of danger. These students can be in a consistent state of awareness, scanning for perceived threats. Seating comfort and lighting/noise comfort are critical in the calming corner. Soft music, to be used with headphones, can provide some level of "distancing" from the stress of the class for some students, and this tool should be available in the calming corner.

- **Establish appropriate time limits:** A calming corner is provided to give students time to use tools to reset their amygdala and reactivate access to their prefrontal cortex. Once students are able to access their prefrontal cortex, they can begin thinking rationally, engage in problem solving, and use creative thinking skills. The amount of time it takes to reset the danger detector in a student's brain can range depending on the student's developmental age and perceived threat. Typically, a two- or three-minute time period in a calming corner is recommended, but this must be flexible. A visual timer without a beeping sound can be a prompt for many students to evaluate their emotional state, but students will need autonomy in advocating for more time as needed.

- **Place tools for relaxation in the corner:** The goal of a calming corner is to provide space for self-regulation and choice. Providing a variety of tools allows students to identify and choose the type of tool that will help them destress, organize their sensory input, self-regulate, and finally return to learning. Various objects can help students reduce their own hypervigilance and stress, and a number of such items should be placed in the calming corner. These might include fidgets, coloring books, noise-canceling headphones, or weighted blankets. These ideas are discussed a bit more in the next section.

- **Teach specific strategies for calming down:** Teachers must teach students how to use a calming corner in order for this strategy to be most effective. Simple breathing techniques (e.g., close your eyes and count 10 breaths slowly, then repeat) offer one relaxation approach, and more ideas for relaxation may be found in Chapter 6.

Grounding Kits

Each child will need different strategies for self-regulation, and any single child may even need different strategies depending on the situation and triggers. One way to support students is to provide a variety of sensory tools for grounding. Because kids exposed to trauma manifest dysregulation, it is not uncommon for their thoughts to be likewise unorganized. In some cases, providing them something to "do with their hands" can help them gain more control over their disorganized thoughts. Many teachers use the idea of grounding kits to help direct the student's attention back to the present moment and the safe environment the child is in. By concentrating on the sensory experiences provided using a grounding tool (e.g., fidget, cloth of different textures), students can move toward a more regulated state by returning to the present.

Grounding kits are merely a collection of such tools and can offer a way to engage one or more of the senses in moments of dysregulation. It is helpful to have grounding kits in the calming corner and perhaps elsewhere in the classroom (e.g., the teacher's desk so the teacher can hand a tool to a student as necessary). Box 4.3 presents several tools that may be included in the grounding kit.

Box 4.3 Creating a grounding kit

Grounding kits are designed to engage students' senses. Teachers should also provide some discussion in the class to ensure that lessons have been provided on how to use the tools provided in the kits.

- Engaging taste—mints, chewing gum, sour candy, crunchy foods like chips
- Engaging touch—stress balls, monkey noodles, putty, slime, water beads, heated and/or weighted stuffed animals
- Engaging smell—scented stickers, scented spray, stuffed animals with essential oils
- Engaging sound—noise-canceling headphones or music options
- Engaging sight—objects that are interesting to hold and look at (gems, heavy and smooth rocks, glitter jars)

It is important to remember that in moments of dysregulation, students will not have high-functioning abilities to answer questions. When a teacher sees that a child is in distress, the teacher should simply place a sensory tool from the grounding kit near the student or consider handing the student one particular tool if it is known what has been supportive for that child in the past. Instead of asking "What would be helpful?" or "Which tool do you want?" simply choose a tool or two and place them near the student. Ensure that the other tools are also readily available, but narrowing down the choices for the child is often helpful in times of dysregulation.

Emotional Thermometer

For sensory supports to be effective, students must learn how to identify their moods and emotions, as well as advocate for their needs in times of distress. While the reason for the dysregulation may be unknown due to fragmented implicit memories, students can learn to identify how their body feels and what would support their self-regulation based on those feelings. Teaching students about their emotions and their ability to self-soothe is aligned with trauma-informed principles of empowerment, such as the effort to strengthen students' voice and choice (Sweetman, 2022).

Students will need lessons designed to help them identify their emotions and how those emotions present in their body. Use of an emotional thermometer can help students move past primary emotions and identify more nuanced descriptions of their feelings. A student feeling distressed might be taught to move out onto a large emotional thermometer on the floor, and thus identify feeling lonely, angry, or afraid. Identifying specific emotions can also help the teacher's response to the student by letting the adult know what may be supportive of the student in that moment. Smaller, handheld emotional thermometers may be developed that identify moods specific for individual children.

Numerous tools are available for emotion identification, from mood wheels to emoji charts (see Chapter 6), and teachers should select the tools appropriate for their students' developmental level. Box 4.4 presents a lesson plan idea using an emotional thermometer.

Box 4.4 Lesson plan on emotional thermometer

This lesson is designed for elementary students in the third through fifth grades. It is best completed in small groups or individually with a guidance counselor. The goal of the lesson is to help the student identify escalating emotions and appropriate regulating tools for each level of emotion intensity. The only tools needed are a blank template of a thermometer, coloring markers, and perhaps pictures from magazines for students to use in making a collage representing various moods.

Begin by identifying the emotion that typically aligns with the student's times of dysregulation. For example, if the pattern of dysregulation aligns with sensory seeking (hitting or pushing), the student may be experiencing sensations of the fight response and may indicate feeling angry or frustrated. If the pattern typically results in sensory-avoidant behaviors (hiding under a table or curling up in a ball), the student may be experiencing sensations of flight and may identify feeling overwhelmed or anxious. The goal is to identify the emotions building up to the highest intensity. If students ultimately experience an intense feeling that overwhelms them, that emotion (a picture representing it) goes at the top of the thermometer. From there, they would identify the emotions leading up to that, which should be less intense. The thermometer may start at the top with *overwhelmed*, followed by *scared*, *anxious*, *worried*, and *insecure*, and the bottom may be *fearful*.

Once the students have identified the feelings words that move in intensity up the thermometer, the teacher might have them color the thermometer or paste on pictures corresponding to those sequenced moods and emotions. *Overwhelmed* at the top may be dark red, and the colors may degrade moving down the thermometer from red to oranges to yellows.

The next step of the lesson is to identify how the body feels when the student is experiencing these emotions. For example, when students are feeling overwhelmed, their bodies may be hot, and students may say they cry and that their hands shake. When students are experiencing worry, they may indicate that they notice they have a nervous stomach. When students are fearful, they may say that they feel uneasy and notice that their eyes are constantly darting around the room. As these students are identifying the way the emotion presents in their body, they should write those terms in the appropriate sections of the thermometer. If the students enjoy art, you can have

(Continued)

(Continued)

them visually represent this (drawing a flame or a tear at the top of the thermometer and eyes at the bottom). Other students may use magazine pictures to make a collage. The final step is to begin identifying a plan for dysregulation. For each emotion on the thermometer, the students will begin to identify what may help them regulate in that moment.

What helps students when they experience "fear" is very different from what may support an "overwhelmed" student. Start this part of the lesson by taking a classroom tour of supports.

Show the students the available tools in the grounding kit such as fidgets, weighted lap blankets, stuffed animals, headphones, or slime. Work with the school to identify resources outside of the classroom like guidance counselors who can remove the student from the classroom or take the student for an active moment such as a walk around the campus. Once the students are aware of their options, have them choose which supports they feel would be most helpful as they experience these various emotions during a day. Remind students that this is a working plan and it can be adjusted as the year progresses.

It is important that all teachers supporting these students are aware of the emotion thermometer and plan. The goal of the thermometer is not only to empower students but to prevent students' explosive moods and emotions from escalating. The student and teacher will work together to identify when a student may be moving up on the thermometer and implement the agreed-upon strategy to de-escalate the student's reaction. All teachers need to be aware of and agree to the plan in order to continue promoting trustworthiness as a principle for a trauma-informed school.

Co-regulation

Co-regulation involves self-regulation, coupled with regulation of others. This process begins in infancy when children are typically exposed to calm, soothing maternal and paternal voices; verbal recognition and validation of distress; and modeling of self-care behaviors. A crying baby is picked up from the crib and held, fed, changed, and rocked. A toddler is soothed after falling down. Experiencing a safe environment where the caregiver is consistently attuned to a child's needs creates a foundation for the growth of self-regulation skills (Murray et al., 2023). Studies show that children who have experienced this type of co-regulation in early childhood will require less co-regulation as they begin to internalize these skills as adolescents and adults (Murray et al., 2023). For many students exposed to trauma, these early co-regulation processes may have been absent or rare during their earliest years.

Studies do suggest that youth who have experienced or are currently experiencing trauma have a heightened need for emotional safety (Murray et al., 2023). Co-regulation provides this emotional safety as students begin to trust that their needs, both physical and emotional, will be met. Consistently offering this safe environment will provide opportunity for students to ultimately learn how to manage their emotions and develop self-regulation skills. Studies are showing that self-regulation skills can be attained throughout the life span and that teaching these skills in later childhood and adolescence is effective for continued growth in students exposed to trauma (Murray et al., 2023; Ouellet et al., 2018).

When working to provide opportunities for co-regulation in the classroom, teachers and administrators should reflect on the ways that co-regulation is offered in infancy and model these behaviors in developmentally appropriate ways. For example, if an infant is crying, the overall goal of the caregiver is to provide a space of calmness so that the infant can manage an overwhelming emotional response. The mother may speak in a calm, soothing voice. The father may provide physical support (nourishment or physical contact). The caregiver may dim the lights or remove a distressing stimulus such as a barking dog or a fire truck siren. These actions validate the infant's distress and teach the child that these needs will be met in a consistent and safe way.

In the classroom, these caregiving behaviors can often be replicated. A teacher can speak in a calm, soothing voice. A teacher can dim the lights or move with the student toward the calming corner to model and engage with physical support from the grounding kit. A teacher can offer nourishment. A teacher can remove the student from the stimulus and have the student walk laps with a paraprofessional or guidance counselor or merely sit outside with a supportive and trained adult. The goal of co-regulation is to consistently model and provide distress management with the student in order for the student to begin to trust that overwhelming emotions can be safely managed. In this manner, over time, students will ultimately learn to better self-regulate.

Instructional Differentiation and Variety

Because of the wide range of sensory issues in different students, teachers will need to employ a wide range of instructional options for these students. While almost all teachers have practiced differentiated instruction for the last two decades, instructional variations are even more critical in the trauma-informed classroom. Both sensory tools, such as those discussed in the grounding kit, and instructional approaches tend to be more varied in a trauma-informed school. Box 4.5 presents additional ideas and suggestions for instructional variation for teachers to consider (Morin, 2023).

Box 4.5 Instructional variations for trauma

- Work with students to develop nonverbal signals they can use when they need a break. Teach them when to use a calming corner, or request help from the teacher, should they feel distressed.
- Develop a "sensory diet"—a tailored plan of physical activities to help kids calm themselves, such as jumping jacks, rolling or therapy balls, push-ups, hopping, using short ladders, or going down slides. Some of these can be done in the back of the class, while others involve playground time.
- Allow a child to use a weighted lap pad, wiggle cushion, or other device approved by an occupational therapist or counselor.
- Let students use technology such as speech-to-text software, spellcheck, or grammar check, as appropriate. These tools can help reduce stress among many students.
- Differentiate lessons, and allow student choice as much as possible between lesson formats. Some students exposed to trauma might prefer to do math practice problems on a computer rather than a worksheet, and software programs typically allow the teacher to select how many such problems are presented on one screen. For some students, limiting the number of problems is a good differentiation technique.

RESEARCH ON EFFICACY OF SENSORY AWARENESS INSTRUCTION

Research on sensory-supportive learning environments is generally supportive of these instructional strategies (Ouellet et al., 2018; Wild & Steeley, 2018). Wild and Steeley (2018) trained teachers in special education classes on the application of a wide array of sensory-supportive teaching techniques, and results showed that students improved in their overall classroom functioning. Thus, students do benefit from a classroom-based sensory program.

In a broader study, Ouellet and colleagues (2018) reviewed the research literature on sensory interventions, and that review showed mixed results. Of the 28 studies reviewed, most showed significant positive impacts of sensory-sensitive techniques, though a small minority of studies did not. Also, the terminology was so varied that general conclusions were not possible across studies. For example, studies involved wide-ranging interventions, including everything from wearing weighted vests to using therapy balls or exercise protocols. With that noted, positive effects were seen in most of the studies reviewed, and in general there is overall support for implementation of sensory-sensitive classroom practices.

A CASE STUDY: TULA'S AGGRESSION

Tula was a student being raised in foster care placement because of abuse in her family home. She was often overstimulated in the classroom and frequently responded by cursing and even displaying aggression, as a result of multiple childhood traumas. For example, sometimes when a school bell rang, or there was a loud shout outside the window, Tula would curse loudly. If another student in class did something unexpected (e.g., dropping a book loudly), Tula would curse at them or toss things at them.

Her fifth-grade teacher, Ms. Ivester, obviously wanted to help Tula gain more control over her behavioral outbursts and curb those behavior problems. She decided to try a simple calming-corner-based intervention to help Tula get more control over her behavior. First, she began to count how many behavioral outbursts or cursing incidents Tula demonstrated each day in her class, and those data are presented in Figure 4.1.

After collecting those baseline data for one week, Ms. Ivester was ready to begin the intervention. Ms. Ivester already had a calming corner established in her class, but she wanted to stress the use of that corner more with the entire class, as well as with Tula. Thus, during morning meeting one day, she motioned to the calming corner and told the class she wanted them to use it a bit more often. She told the class that whenever someone felt angry or had their feelings hurt, they had the right to go sit in the calming corner, either on the chair or on the rug, for several minutes and use the items in the grounding kit located there to help them calm down. Ms. Ivester stated that no more than one person could be in the corner at any one time.

The class was told that, when someone was in the corner, no one else should bother them. Finally, the students were told that after the two- or three-minute "calm down" period, Ms. Ivester would speak to them and remind them to come back to class, if they felt that they could. She told them they could use the calming corner when they needed to, but that they were not allowed to overuse

Figure 4.1 • *Tula's misbehaviors*

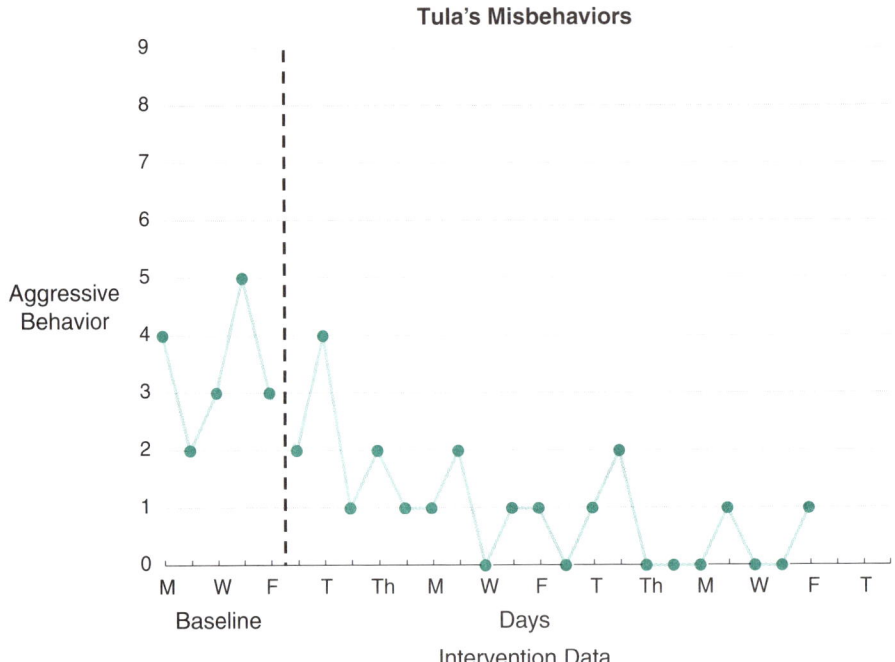

it! She also let them know that if she saw them getting angry, she, as the teacher, would request that they go to the calming corner before a behavioral infraction occurred. These instructions were provided for the entire class after Ms. Ivester had collected baseline behavioral data on Tula.

Then, at the end of class that same day, Ms. Ivester asked to speak privately to Tula. She told her the following:

> Tula, I can see that sometimes you get upset when other people say something to you, or you hear a loud noise. Sometimes you even get mad and curse at them or hit them. You remember when we talked about our lizard brains sometimes taking over our thoughts, and keeping us angry? Sometimes, your lizard brain gets you into trouble, and of course, when you hit someone, I have to respond by implementing consequences. I was thinking that if you use the calming corner when you begin to feel angry, or get your feelings hurt, you can avoid consequences. If you feel your lizard brain begin to take over, you can just get up from your desk, walk back there, and sit down, and no one will bother you for a bit. Do you think you can do that?

In this example, these simple instructions were all it took to help Tula begin to effectively self-regulate her anger and curb her aggression that very day. The behavioral outbursts decreased from more than three per day (an average of 3.4 per day, during the first week) to only two during the final week. This was a huge success for this intervention, and certainly helped Tula feel more successful in self-regulating her emotions. It also made the class much more enjoyable for Ms. Ivester! Also, this intervention provided behavioral data that Ms. Ivester could share with Tula, stressing that Tula had learned to use her smart part to control her own behavior. Sharing this type of success with students can be critical in their overwhelming need to control themselves and their environment.

SUMMARY

Some difficulty in processing sensory information is expected when students are exposed to trauma, and teachers in the trauma-informed school must be prepared to deal with these issues. Several times in this chapter, we have mentioned that a wide array of sensory issues necessitates a wide array of instructional options for teachers to use. While sensory issues can often be challenging, many times these concerns can be dealt with using fairly simple instructional practices (e.g., fidget, calming corner, alternative seating). Other times, as in the case study about Tula, a simple instructional intervention may be required. What is certain is that sensory issues stemming from trauma are likely to result in dysregulation of moods, emotions, and behaviors for these children, and preparing in advance for these issues is paramount in the trauma-informed classroom.

REFERENCES

Craig, S. (2017). *Trauma-informed schools: Specific classroom strategies* [Audio interview]. Educator Summit 2017. Retrieved from https://www.attachmen ttraumanetwork.org/atn-store-educator-2017-summit/

Joseph, R. Y., Casteleijn, D., van der Linde, J., & Franzsen, D. (2021). Sensory modulation dysfunction in child victims of trauma: A scoping review. *Journal of Child Adolescent Trauma, 14*(4), 455–470.

Margolin, G., & Vickerman, K. (2007). Post-traumatic stress in children and adolescents exposed to family violence: Overview and issues. *Professional Psychology: Research and Practice, 38*(6), 613–619.

Morin, A. (2023, October 20). Classroom accommodations for sensory processing challenges. Understood. Retrieved from https://www.under stood.org/articles/classroom-accommodations-for-sensory-processing-challenges

Murray, D. W., Rackers, H., Meyer, A., McKenzie, K. J., Malm, K., Sepulveda, K., & Heath, C. (2023). Co-regulation as a support for older youth in the context of foster care: A scoping review of the literature. *Prevention Science*, *24*(6), 1187–1197. Retrieved from https://www.doi.org/10.1007/s11121-023-01531-3

Noddings, A. (2017). Classroom solutions for sensory sensitive students. *American Montessori Society*. Retrieved from https://amshq.org/About-Montessori/Montessori-Articles/All-Articles/Classroom-Solutions-for-Sensory-Sensitive-Students

Ouellet, B., Carreau, E., Dion, V., Rouat, A., Tremblay, E., & Voisin, J. I. A. (2018). Efficacy of sensory interventions on school participation of children with sensory disorders: A systematic review. *American Journal of Lifestyle Medicine*, *15*(1), 75–83.

Perry, B. D. (2000). Traumatized children: How childhood trauma influences brain development. *Journal of the California Alliance for the Mentally Ill*, *11*(1), 48–51.

Perry, B. D. (2014). *Helping traumatized children: A brief overview for caregivers*. ChildTrauma Academy. Retrieved from https://www.child trauma.org/_files/ugd/aa51c7_237459a7e16b4b7e9d2c4837c908eefe.pdf

Robinson, C., & Brown, A. M. (2016). Considering sensory processing issues in trauma affected children: The physical environment in children's residential homes. *Scottish Journal of Residential Child Care*, *15*(1). Retrieved from https://www.celcis.org/application/files/8316/2308/6835/002._2016_Vol_15_1_Robinson_Considering_Sensory_Processing.pdf

Schaff, R., Benevides, T., Imperatore Blanche, E., Brett-Green, B. A., Burke, J. P., Cohn, E. S., . . . Schoen, S. A. (2010). Parasympathetic functions in children with sensory processing disorder. *Frontiers in Integrative Neuroscience*, *4*. Retrieved from https://www.frontiersin.org/articles/10.3389/fnint.2010.00004/full

Sweetman, N. (2022). What is a trauma-informed classroom? What are the benefits and challenges involved? *Frontiers in Education*, *7*. Retrieved from https://www.frontiersin.org/articles/10.3389/feduc.2022.914448/full

van der Kolk, B. A. (2014). *The body keeps the score: Mind, brain and body in the transformation of trauma*. Allen Lane—Penguin Books.

Wild, G., & Steeley, S. L. (2018). A model for classroom-based intervention for children with sensory processing differences. *International Journal of Special Education*, *33*(3). Retrieved from https://files.eric.ed.gov/fulltext/EJ1196698.pdf

Winterbottom, M., & Wilkins, A. (2009). Lighting and discomfort in the classroom. *Journal of Environmental Psychology*, 29(1), 63–75. Retrieved from https://www.sciencedirect.com/science/article/abs/pii/S027249 4408001011

CHAPTER 5

SOCIAL-EMOTIONAL LEARNING

THE BASICS OF SOCIAL-EMOTIONAL LEARNING

Social-emotional learning (SEL) includes a number of emphases, and different proponents provide varying perspectives on what SEL actually is (Adams, 2014; Craig, 2017; Goleman, 1995; Lippman & Schmitz, 2013; Simmons-Duffin, 2018). Programs range from social skills programs (Cooke et al., 2007) to meditation programs (Black, Milam, & Sussman, 2009), and all are considered variations of SEL (Durlak, Weissberg, Dymnicki, Taylor, & Schellinger, 2011; Vega, 2017). Still, undergirding the SEL construct are at least two emphases, emotional intelligence and resilience. Each of these is a critical concern for students exposed to trauma.

Emotional Intelligence

Beginning with Daniel Goleman's 1995 book, *Emotional Intelligence*, schools in the United States and around the world have placed more emphasis on developing the child socially and emotionally. In Goleman's view, highly developed SEL skills, such as empathy, interpretation of social cues, and the ability to identify one's own emotions and ultimately exert control over them via self-regulation, are defined as "emotional intelligence." His central thesis was that emotional intelligence probably impacts overall success in life more than either IQ or academic ability, since one's ability to self-regulate emotions and get along well with others often dictates one's success in the working environment as well as in all social relationships. This was a new emphasis for educators in 1995 when this book first appeared, as IQ and academic success had been "coins of the realm" in education for nearly a century.

Emotional intelligence is often defined as the capability of individuals to recognize and self-regulate their own moods and emotions, as well as to recognize the emotions and moods of others, coupled with the capability to use this knowledge to guide their thinking and behavior to facilitate their efficacy in life (Goleman, 1995). In this definition, one can see the numerous implications for kids exposed to trauma, whose strongest motivation is often to develop increased self-efficacy and control over their own life situation. As this concept of emotional intelligence took root in education, schools began to look for ways to help students enhance skills in this vast array of areas.

Of note in this definition is the rather elastic nature of the SEL concept. Because of this all-encompassing nature of the construct, the supporting research includes everything from evaluation of social skills programs to mood awareness activities in kindergarten. Despite this broad nature, the instructional approach is useful for determining how to assist kids repeatedly exposed to trauma, who typically manifest significant deficits in many areas.

Resilience

More recently, in considering how to teach children and adolescents exposed to trauma, or those manifesting other significant behavioral problems, the concept of resilience has grown in influence (Lippman & Schmitz, 2013). Resilience, in the most basic sense, is one's ability to bounce back from negative life circumstances, and while developed among psychologists and educators to help children with abnormal behaviors or emotional problems, this idea is now guiding much of the thinking when it comes to children exposed to trauma as well. Many factors can help kids bounce back from less-than-adequate life circumstances, and psychologists have used the term *resilience factors* to describe these things that can potentially foster resilience. In particular, resilience factors tend to offset the impact of exposure to adverse childhood experiences (ACEs), such that the negatives associated with such exposure are minimized. Thus, if exposure to multiple ACEs represents the "bad news" of childhood trauma, resilience factors represent the "good news." Resilience factors over time actually help to reprogram the neuronal connections in the child's brain, fostering more positive thought processes not based on lizard brain responses. According to Lippman and Schmitz (2013), individual resilience factors include all of the following:

- Physical health supports, including getting enough sleep, eating well, exercising, and enjoying good health

▸ Social and emotional competencies, including stress management; a sense of control over one's life; a positive relationship to self, such as a sense of self-efficacy, self-regulation, and self-esteem; and hopefulness and goal setting, with both the motivation to succeed and the perseverance needed to reach those goals

▸ Cognitive competencies, including insightfulness and general skills such as problem solving, information processing, and intellectual ability

Coupled with these individual attributes, the researchers likewise emphasized a variety of outside supports, within either the family or the community, that will help foster resilience (Lippman & Schmitz, 2013). These include a supportive family; exposure to parents or caregivers with effective parenting skills; the presence of a caring adult outside the family, such as a teacher, coach, or counselor; and membership in various social organizations, such as school clubs, scouts, or age-appropriate religious groups (Adams, 2014; Lippman & Schmitz, 2013; Simmons-Duffin, 2018).

Given this array of resilience factors, one can note the appropriateness of using the concept of resilience in relation to students exposed to repeated trauma. In fact, the resilience factors listed earlier read like a litany of life circumstances that are generally absent in the early lives of many children exposed to trauma. Of course, some of these factors can be addressed by the schools, whereas others cannot. Although educators do play a role (as discussed in Chapter 1) in watching for and identifying some forms of childhood trauma, such as child sex abuse or neglect, they are virtually powerless when it comes to protecting children from other risk factors (e.g., poverty or dysfunctional parenting in the home environment). Still, research on childhood resilience has shown that one caring adult in the community can be the resilience factor that allows a child to succeed even when exposed to several ACEs (Felitti et al., 1998; Lippman & Schmitz, 2013). Clearly, schools can and often do provide such an adult role model for at-risk children, and a subsequent strategy in this book, adult mentoring (discussed in Chapter 9), will focus on fostering childhood resilience in exactly that fashion.

Finally, we should note that this resilience concept fits nicely with the idea of emotional intelligence. For both adults and school students, developing emotional intelligence facilitates the ability to empathize with others and to use that empathy to better interpret and navigate emotional and social interactions with peers. The literature on this concept stresses that these skills will lead to increased success in life for all students. However, from the perspective of children exposed to trauma, emotional intelligence can be seen as even more critical, because developing these skills will, in all likelihood, fill a deficit of such skills.

SOCIAL-EMOTIONAL LEARNING

Based on both emotional intelligence and resilience constructs, SEL is a concept and a movement in psychology and education stressing emotional and mental health as critically important for students' long-term development and overall success in life (Belfield et al., 2015; Craig, 2017; Goleman, 1995; Lippman & Schmitz, 2013). SEL is the effort to develop students' knowledge and skills in managing emotions, building healthy relationships, developing positive social skills and relationships, building resiliency, and making good life choices regarding participation in risky behaviors such as early sexual experiences, bullying, and drug abuse (Belfield et al., 2015).

In addition to this definition, most authors in this area stress five key competencies as the primary bases for SEL (Durlak et al., 2011; Shriver & Bridgeland, 2015; Taylor, Oberle, Durlak, & Weissberg, 2017; Vega, 2017). A quick review of those key competencies will, once again, show the broad nature of the SEL concept. The key competencies, as summarized by Vega (2017), are presented in Box 5.1.

Box 5.1 Key competencies for social-emotional learning

- Self-Awareness
  - What are my thoughts and feelings?
  - What causes those thoughts and feelings?
  - How can I express my thoughts and feelings respectfully?
- Self-Management
  - What different responses can I have to an event?
  - How can I respond to an event as constructively as possible?
- Social Awareness
  - How can I better understand other people's thoughts and feelings?
  - How can I better understand why people feel and think the way they do?
- Relationship Skills
  - How can I adjust my actions so that my interactions with others turn out well?
  - How can I communicate my expectations to other people?
  - How can I communicate with others so that they understand and manage their expectations of me?
- Responsible Decision Making
  - What consequences will my actions have for myself and others?
  - How do my choices align with my values?
  - How can I solve problems creatively?

Given these broad competencies, educators will quickly realize that this concept of SEL encompasses many individual skills not included in the traditional school curriculum. Further, these competencies may be taught with a variety of techniques ranging from in-class discussions of moods and emotions to service-learning programs within the community. Here are several simple SEL teaching ideas.

Mood Wheels

Helping young children become aware of their moods and emotions is the first step in helping those children self-regulate moods, emotions, and behavior. Some kindergarten and early elementary teachers use a "mood wheel" to help students understand their different moods, as shown in Figure 5.1. This mood wheel may be easily constructed using laminated paper for the wheel itself, on which the teacher writes down words representing different moods or emotions (*angry*, *depressed*, *fearful*, *uncomfortable*, *happy*, *excited*, *very interested*, etc.).

For young children in the pre-reading years, an emoji may be pictured on the wheel beside the term itself. Another sheet of laminated paper with a picture of a selection arrow could then be affixed to the wheel, allowing children to

Figure 5.1 • *A mood wheel*

Social-Emotional Learning

spin the wheel to select the emotion or mood they are feeling at that moment. Also, teachers can find more information on mood wheels and even download a printable wheel from the following site: https://childhood101.com/helping-children-manage-big-emotions-my-emotions-wheel-printable/.

Teachers may use a wheel at each child's desk or one large wheel at the front of the room (or both). If each child has a mood wheel, the teacher can instruct all students to identify their mood first thing in the morning and leave the wheel visible on their desk. Then, should that mood change, the children should be encouraged to reset the mood wheel to reflect their changed mood. At any point, should individual children indicate they are angry or very depressed, the teacher should make time to have a quick discussion with them to see what the problem might be. The purpose here is not to do in-depth therapy with every mood change but merely to get children used to identifying and labeling their own moods and emotions. This is, of course, the first step to controlling them.

Anger Thermometer

The anger thermometer is a variation of the emotional thermometer idea introduced in Chapter 4. Sousa (2009) provided an example of an anger thermometer describing moods on a prioritized scale ranging from "Feeling peaceful and ready to work" to "Feeling angry and too upset to do anything." Another example is shown in Figure 5.2, and kids can show their level of anger by moving a paper clip from one level to the next.

When explaining the anger thermometer to students, the teacher might state that students can choose, to some degree, what they feel, and that feeling frustrated is less intense than feeling angry. Teachers could then suggest that feeling frustrated rather than angry may give the child more control over a given situation, and at the very least having children label and discuss their feelings heightens awareness of them. Being invited to describe their moods as progressive states can help even very young children understand that moods and emotions sometimes build upon each other. Again, this discussion will tend to build some self-control by cautioning participants to not jump immediately into anger and rage. Such activities allow students to assess their own moods and emotions and ultimately gain control over them, resulting in improved self-regulation of moods and decreased anger and aggression (Davis, 2015).

Figure 5.2 • *Anger thermometer*

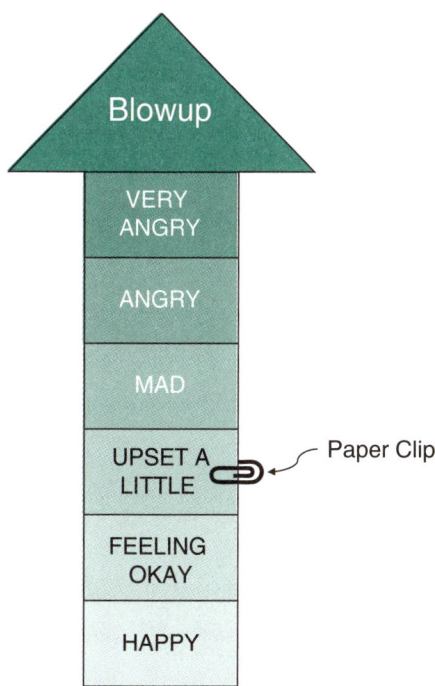

PUBLISHED PROGRAMS AND CURRICULA

There is a wide array of published curricula designed to assist in SEL instruction, and a brief discussion of several of these should help in understanding the emphases that SEL involves (Belfield et al., 2015; Cooke et al., 2007; Upshur, Heyman, & Wenz-Gross, 2017). Two of the most used curricula are discussed in this section. Also, the website companion to this book includes a brief review of several other SEL curricula.

Second Step

One curriculum that has been the focus of SEL research is Second Step. As described by Cooke et al. (2007), the Second Step curriculum emphasizes the following skills:

1. **Impulse control**—the ability to control and manage thoughts, feelings, and behaviors, including listening, focusing attention, following directions, using self-talk, showing assertiveness, and identifying and understanding feelings

2. **Empathy**—use of appropriate conversation skills, joining groups, and making friends

3. **Emotional management**—ability to calm oneself; manage anger; deal effectively with accusations, disappointment, and anxious or hurt feelings; resist revenge; and avoid jumping to conclusions

4. **Problem solving**—the ability to play fairly, take responsibility, solve classroom problems, solve peer exclusion problems, handle name-calling, deal with peer pressure or gossip, and seek help when needed

As these areas indicate, this program is comprehensive and addresses many of the key competencies that define SEL. Implementation of Second Step usually involves a schoolwide effort and includes both teacher and parent training elements. Programs are available for early learning, elementary school, and middle school, and the Second Step program has been implemented in more than 26,000 schools worldwide. The class activities are available with each component of Second Step and easily used in any classroom. Also, research cited on the company website as well as in numerous academic journals is strongly supportive of this program (Espelage, Low, Polanin, & Brown, 2013; Low, Cook, Smolkowski, & Buntain-Ricklefs, 2015; Upshur et al., 2017).

Responsive Classroom and Morning Meetings

Another commonly used SEL program is the Responsive Classroom, intended for use with K–5 students. Using this program will help students monitor and self-regulate their moods, emotions, and behaviors, and this tends to increase academic learning (Center for Responsive Schools, 2017; Kriete & Davis, 2014; see also www.responsiveclassroom.org). The program also builds students' self-confidence and gives them problem-solving skills that they can utilize in and out of the classroom as well as into their lives beyond school. Each of these emphases is critical for students exposed to trauma.

There are five parts to the Responsive Classroom approach in elementary school: establishing rules, morning meeting, energizers, quiet time, and closing circle. Students exposed to trauma need increased control, and in the Responsive Classroom, students help to establish the rules for the class. As a class, students create three or four rules that will help them to reach their goals. The identified rules are agreed upon and then written on a poster that is signed by all the students and the teacher. This poster should be displayed in the classroom and referred to often. Students exposed to trauma need consistency in rule application and a personal sense of ownership of the rules, both of which are emphasized in this curriculum.

Perhaps the best-known feature of the Responsive Classroom is the morning meeting. This classwide activity involves four parts: a greeting phase, a sharing time, a group activity, and the morning message (Bruce, Fasy, Gulick, Jones, & Pike, 2006; Kriete & Davis, 2014). The intent of the greeting is to set a positive tone for the day and provide a sense of recognition for each student. Students are given opportunities to look one another in the eye, shake hands, and use each other's names. This encourages the social interaction that many students exposed to trauma need. The sharing portion of the meeting involves questions that everyone responds to, to help develop social understanding and help students think about and articulate their thoughts. The goal of the group activity is to build a positive sense of community, typically by singing songs or playing games together. The morning message is a place where the teacher leads a short discussion. Teachers may then review any upcoming activities, review classroom rules, problem solve relative to a previous event or problem in the class, or discuss any emotional struggles that students are having (Bruce et al., 2006). Again, this emphasizes the importance of community discussions of problems and possible solutions to conflict.

While extensive reviews of curricula are not a focus of this text, we should point out that research regarding the Responsive Classroom approach has shown many positive impacts in terms of increased self-regulation, mood control, and improved behavior (Bruce et al., 2006; Durlak et al., 2011; Rimm-Kaufman, 2004; Rimm-Kaufman, Fan, Chiu, & You, 2007; Vega, 2017). Again, this curricula emphasizes many things needed by children exposed to trauma.

RESEARCH ON SOCIAL-EMOTIONAL LEARNING

Almost all of the considerable body of research on SEL investigated the implementation of commercially available SEL curricula, rather than individual teacher-developed SEL activities such as the use of mood wheels. Still, the research on social-emotional interventions overall is quite positive and clearly shows that SEL works (Belfield et al., 2015; Cooke et al., 2007; Dodge et al., 2014; Durlak et al., 2011; Espelage et al., 2013; Jones, Brown, & Aber, 2011; Low et al., 2015; Shriver & Bridgeland, 2015; Taylor et al., 2017; Upshur et al., 2017; Vega, 2017).

For example, research that investigated the impact of SEL on academic performance. showed a positive impact (Belfield et al., 2015; Durlak et al., 2011; Jones et al., 2011; Taylor et al., 2017; Vega, 2017). In fact, one meta-analysis of 213 SEL programs found that social and emotional learning interventions increased students' academic performance by 11 percentile points (Durlak et al., 2011). The research also supports the use of SEL curricula to improve behavior and decrease depression, anxiety, and aggression (Belfield et al., 2015; Durlak et al., 201l; Taylor et al., 2017). As noted in previous chapters, these are target behaviors of students exposed to trauma.

Other research on SEL shows significant benefits in additional areas that are crucially important for children exposed to trauma. For example, SEL training can help students develop empathy for others, improve attitudes toward others, improve regulation of moods, and decrease drug usage and other risky behaviors many years after the program is implemented (Dodge et al., 2014; Durlak et al., 2011; Jones et al., 2011; Taylor et al., 2017). In fact, a number of studies have shown rather robust, long-term impacts of social-emotional training (Dodge et al., 2014; Jones et al., 2011; Taylor et al., 2017), suggesting that positive impacts of social-emotional training can be seen years after these school-based interventions conclude. These studies show benefits in terms of less illegal drug use, fewer social-emotional problems, and improved interpersonal skills (Dodge et al., 2014; Taylor et al., 2017). As one example, Dodge et al. (2014) studied 25-year-old former students who had received some form of SEL during their school years. The results showed that these young adults were 10% less likely than others to demonstrate psychological, behavioral, or substance abuse problems.

In a rather unusual research analysis, Belfield et al. (2015) investigated the economic impact of SEL interventions in a cost-benefit analysis—a type of research that is extremely uncommon in educational literature. Results showed that, on average for every dollar spent on social-emotional interventions, there was a return of $11 over the early years of the young adults' lives. This type of long-term follow-up is quite rare in most educational intervention research, and strongly indicates that schools should be emphasizing SEL instruction for all students.

A CASE STUDY ON SOCIAL-EMOTIONAL LEARNING

Ms. Kay was very concerned about a child, Austin, in her fourth-grade class. He seemed to get frustrated and then angry virtually every day, and once he felt anger, he seemed to lose control of his emotions. His behavior became extreme and sometimes violent at that point. She was unaware of any specific concerns in his home environment, but clearly, he was not as emotionally literate as her other students in labeling and understanding his own emotions. Further, he seemed unable to regulate his emotional outbursts. He often ended up crying, and sometimes he began to hit students near him. Finally, he could get angry at almost anything, from not knowing the answer to a question, to a student across the room making a loud noise. Ms. Kay was not in a school that had implemented a schoolwide SEL program, so any intervention she chose to implement meant working on Austin's problems alone.

Still, Ms. Kay wanted an intervention that would help Austin identify, understand, and ultimately control his emotions, so she decided to use a simple social-emotional intervention discussed previously, the mood wheel. To begin, she kept a count of each instance in which Austin lost control of his moods and had to be called out for disciplinary reasons in class each day. She collected these baseline data for a week, as shown in Figure 5.3.

Figure 5.3 • *Mood wheel intervention data for Austin*

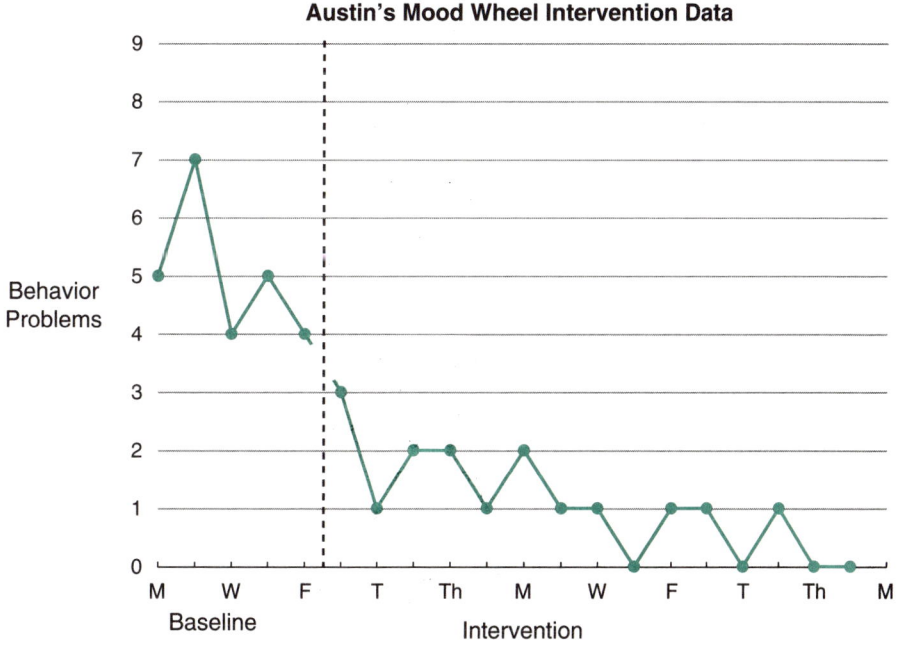

Next, to begin the mood wheel intervention, she made a large mood wheel for the entire class, and discussed the moods presented on the wheel with the students. She chose the following mood indicators:

- Feeling just okay
- Happy
- Excited and ready to learn
- Mildly upset about something
- Very upset
- Frustrated
- Angry
- Calming down

On the first intervention day, the class talked about the feelings that indicated particular moods and some of the things that might move kids toward one mood or another. Then, Ms. Kay made five "student-sized" mood wheels and explained that each week, five different students would use the mood wheels. Each time their mood changed during the day, they would indicate that new mood on the mood wheel, and, if Ms. Kay decided it was appropriate, the class would then briefly discuss that child's mood change.

With multiple students using the individual mood wheels, Austin was not particularly singled out in front of the class, but Ms. Kay made certain that Austin was in the first group of five students to use the mood wheel. Each morning, all five of the students were asked to set their mood wheels at "Excited and ready to learn" unless they felt something else. They were then told to reset their mood wheels when they felt a mood change and hold them up for Ms. Kay to see. She could then determine if the class should discuss the mood change, depending on classwork and other factors.

For Austin, Ms. Kay did not count the number of times his mood changed during a given day. Rather, she counted the number of times he showed angry or disruptive behavior overall, regardless of whether he used the mood wheel to label his mood change. With all five of the students, she made a point of discussing some of the mood changes, depending on the importance of the mood change, the time, and ongoing activities in her class.

After the first week, Ms. Kay explained to the class that two of the five students using the mood wheel had done so well with it that they would continue to use the wheel, while the other three students would pass their mood wheel along to someone else. In that way, Austin and another student continued to use the mood wheel for a second week.

These data show that during the first week, Austin began to reduce the number of times he showed anger, and by the second week, his anger outbursts were significantly reduced. He had gone from an average of five outbursts daily to fewer than two, and Ms. Kay was particularly pleased to reach the afternoon on Thursday during the second intervention week and realize that she'd had no behavioral problems from Austin all that day!

Of course, this intervention did not eliminate Austin's behavioral problems, nor did it address his long-term emotional needs. However, it did make him much more "teachable" in the classroom, and often that type of small victory can be the basis for establishing lasting trust with students exposed to trauma. As noted previously for these children, all victories count!

SUMMARY

SEL has gone far beyond merely an instructional approach to assist with troubled kids and has now become a "cause" for many educators. When we consider the number of students exposed to trauma in schools today, we can easily understand why. As this brief summary shows, the research is strongly supportive of SEL, and while the overall SEL area is quite broad, schools are lining up, and linking up, to create SEL school networks. At the very least, these innovative programs provide a way for schools to address behavioral problems for many students, and SEL training shows the most potential to address the critical needs of kids exposed to trauma in schools today. For this reason, we might well expect some type of SEL implementation in virtually all schools at some point in the near future. Clearly, absent such an effort, schools will not be meeting the needs of many children, and particularly the needs of children exposed to trauma.

REFERENCES

Adams, J. M. (2014, February 3). New "trauma-informed" approach to behavioral disorders in special education. *EdSource*. Retrieved from https://edsource.org/2014/new-trauma-informed-approach-to-behavioral-disorders-in-special-education/56753

Belfield, C., Bowden, B., Klapp, A., Levin, H., Shand, R., & Zander, S. (2015). *The economic value of social emotional learning*. Columbia University.

Black, D. S., Milam, J., & Sussman, S. (2009). Sitting meditation interventions among youth: A review of treatment efficacy. *Pediatrics, 124*, 532–541.

Bruce, S., Fasy, C., Gulick, J., Jones, J., & Pike, E. (2006). Making morning circle meaningful. *Teaching Exceptional Children Plus, 2*(4), 1–9.

Center for Responsive Schools. (2017). *Responsive classroom course for elementary educators: Resource book*. Center for Responsive Schools.

Cooke, M. B., Ford, J., Levine, J., Bourke, C., Newell, L., & Lapidus, G. (2007). The effects of city-wide implementation of "Second Step" on elementary school students' pro-social and aggressive behaviors. *Journal of Primary Prevention, 28*(2), 93–115.

Craig, S. (2017). *Trauma-informed schools: Specific classroom strategies*. [Audio interview]. Educator Summit 2017. Retrieved from https://www.attachmen ttraumanetwork.org/atn-store-educator-2017-summit/

Davis, L. C. (2015, August 31). When mindfulness meets the classroom. *The Atlantic*. Retrieved from https://www.theatlantic.com/education/archive/ 2015/08/mindfulness-education-schools-meditation/402469/

Dodge, K. A., Bierman, K. L., Coie, J. D., Greenberg, M. T., Lochman, J. E., McMahon, R. J., & Pinderhughes, E. E. (2014). Impact of early intervention on psychopathology, crime, and well-being at age 25. *American Journal of Psychiatry, 172*(1), 59–70.

Durlak, J., Weissberg, R. P., Dymnicki, A. B., Taylor, R. D., & Schellinger, K. B. (2011). The impact of enhancing students' social and emotional learning: A meta-analysis of school-based universal interventions. *Child Development, 82*(1), 405–432.

Espelage, D. L., Low, S., Polanin, J. R., & Brown, E. C. (2013). The impact of a middle school program to reduce aggression, victimization, and sexual violence. *Journal of Adolescent Health, 53*(2), 180–186.

Felitti, V., Anda, R. F., Nordenberg, D., Williamson, D. F., Spitz, A. M., Edwards, V., & Marks, J. S. (1998). Relationship of childhood abuse and household dysfunction to many of the leading causes of death in adults. *American Journal of Preventive Medicine, 14*, 245–258.

Goleman, D. (1995). *Emotional intelligence: Why it can matter more than IQ*. New York, NY: Bantam Books.

Jones, S. M., Brown, J. I., & Aber, J. L. (2011). Two-year impacts of a universal school-based social-emotional and literacy intervention: An experiment in translational developmental research. *Child Development, 82*(2), 533–554.

Kriete, R., & Davis, C. (2014). The morning meeting book. *Young Children, 58*(1), 96.

Lippman, L., & Schmitz, H. (2013, October 30). *What can schools due to build resilience in their students?* Child Trends. Retrieved from https://www. childtrends.org/what-can-schools-do-to-build-resilience-in-their-students

Low, S., Cook, C. R., Smolkowski, K., & Buntain-Ricklefs, J. (2015). Promoting social-emotional competence: An evaluation of the elementary version of Second Step. *Journal of School Psychology*, *53*, 463–477.

Rimm-Kaufman, S. E. (2004). Primary-grade teachers' self-efficacy beliefs, attitudes toward teaching, and discipline and teaching practice priorities in relation to the Responsive Classroom approach: Social and academic learning study—A three year longitudinal study of the Responsive Classroom approach. *The Elementary School Journal*, *104*(4), 1–4.

Rimm-Kaufman, S., Fan, X., Chiu, Y., & You, W. (2007). The contribution of the responsive classroom approach on children's academic achievement: Results from a three year longitudinal study. *Journal of School Psychology*, *45*, 401–421. Retrieved from https://www.doi.org/10.1016/j.jsp.2006.10.003

Shriver, T. P., & Bridgeland, J. M. (2015, February 26). Social-emotional learning pays off. *Education Week*. Retrieved from https://www.edweek.org/ew/articles/2015/02/26/social-emotional-learning-pays-off.html

Simmons-Duffin, S. (2018, May 23). To teach kids to handle tough emotions, some schools take time out for group therapy. In *All things considered*. NPR. Retrieved from https://www.npr.org/sections/health-shots/2018/05/23/613465023/for-troubled-kids-some-schools-take-time-out-for-group-therapy

Sousa, D. A. (2009). *How the brain influences behavior: Management strategies for every classroom*. Corwin.

Taylor, R. D., Oberle, E., Durlak, J. A., & Weissberg, R. P. (2017). Promoting positive youth development through school-based social and emotional learning interventions: A meta-analysis of follow-up effects. *Child Development*, *88*(4), 1156–1171.

Upshur, C. C., Heyman, M., & Wenz-Gross, M. (2017). Efficacy trail of the Second Step Early Learning (SSEL) curriculum: Preliminary outcomes. *Journal of Applied Developmental Psychology*, *50*, 15–25.

Vega, V. (2017, June 14). Social and emotional learning research review. *Edutopia*. Retrieved from https://www.edutopia.org/sel-research-learning-outcomes

CHAPTER 6

MINDFULNESS AND RELAXATION STRATEGIES

Professionals and clinicians have long noted the need to help students alleviate stress and regulate their moods as an intervention for a wide variety of emotional problems and behavioral problems in the classroom (Ackerman, 2018; Felver et al., 2022; Quirk, 2023; Schneider, 1974; Semple, Reid, & Miller, 2005; Thomas, 2016). However, with recent data showing that the COVID-19 pandemic was "devastating for the mental health of teens" because of the increased stress associated with the social isolation of that period (Quirk, 2023), mindfulness and relaxation strategies have taken on additional importance. Thus, not only students exposed to trauma but almost all students can benefit from stress reduction practices. For students exposed to trauma, however, a strategy that helps them reduce stress and learn to control their moods and emotions is, perhaps, even more critical.

Historically, both relaxation and mindfulness strategies have been used to empower students in schools, in clinical practice, and at home to control their stress and their moods, as well as to de-escalate highly charged emotional situations. Research presented throughout this chapter will show the efficacy of each (Ackerman, 2018; Felver et al., 2022). Thus, we urge all school faculty to implement one or the other of these interventions, and that can be accomplished either as a schoolwide intervention or teacher by teacher. These tools are also useful for parents or caregivers of students exposed to trauma.

MINDFULNESS

Because children exposed to trauma manifest various mood disorders, difficulties with emotion regulation, and other behavioral concerns, helping these students understand that they can gain some control over their own moods and emotions can be one of the most important things we teach them.

Again, teaching students to identify ways to control themselves and their environment is an integral component of a trauma-informed classroom. In fact, such emotional self-regulation skills may be much more important for their long-term success than almost anything else in the school curriculum. We only need to consider one question: "What good will total mastery of the school curriculum do for students exposed to extensive trauma if they are still consistently dysregulated?"

The growing mindfulness movement among schools worldwide provides an excellent teaching strategy that addresses many of these mood difficulties, emotional concerns, and even the classroom behavioral problems of children exposed to trauma. With roots in both yoga and certain Buddhist meditation practices, mindfulness has become a widely accepted intervention strategy in schools throughout the United States, as well as the United Kingdom and worldwide. Further, many trauma-informed schools specifically implement some type of mindfulness program as one aspect of helping students impacted by trauma, while realizing that mindfulness serves all children and adolescents in today's post-COVID-19 world.

The most common type of mindfulness strategy involves providing students with a meditative time period during which they reflect on their breathing to increase their level of relaxation. In turn, this stress reduction can result in reduced depression and anxiety, as well as increased student attention and improved classroom behavior (Campbell, 2013; Davis, 2015; Felver et al., 2022; Klatta, Harpsterb, Brownea, White, & Case-Smith, 2013). Mindfulness also stresses recognition of and control over one's emotional states and moods, and thus mindfulness practices are aimed directly at self-regulation (Albrecht, Albrecht, & Cohen, 2012).

Using mindfulness exercises, educators and, in many cases, parents can teach students of all ages to assess and regulate their own emotional state, to calm themselves down, to concentrate on one thing at a time, and to reflect more deeply on their work (Albrecht et al., 2012; Harris, 2015). Students can learn mindfulness techniques in as little as 15 minutes daily over a period of six to eight weeks, and such practices ultimately will have many benefits that directly address the many aberrant behaviors and emotional problems demonstrated by children exposed to trauma.

To actually see mindfulness exercises in real classrooms, we suggest that readers view one or more of the many YouTube videos on mindfulness in schools (a number of which are listed on the companion website for this book:

https://traumahelpnow.com). Several mindfulness curricula are available for teachers (also described on the website); however, teachers should bear in mind that they can undertake implementation of mindfulness, without using these curricula, by reviewing the free materials from YouTube, this book, and other such free resources. Again, the companion website for this book (https://traumahelpnow.com) provides many other resources and videos on mindfulness used from elementary school through high school.

While mindfulness practices may seem somewhat esoteric, or perhaps even a bit "new age" to some veteran teachers, the practice has been expanding in schools around the world for one reason; it works! This practice seems to help all children and adolescents in school focus more, and thus mindfulness has benefits far beyond those that may be accomplished for students exposed to trauma.

Mindfulness practices evolved from yoga in the early 1970s as a way to boost energy and productivity (Davis, 2015). Mindfulness has since been employed by many organizations including Google, the U.S. Army, and the Seattle Seahawks football team (Davis, 2015), and today, many educators are implementing daily mindfulness exercises in the classroom (Felver et al., 2022; Greenberg & Harris, 2012; Oaklander, 2015). Given this rather wide acceptance of mindfulness to help individuals regulate their emotions and reduce stress, mindfulness is certainly something that can be recommended for all students exposed to trauma, as well as for others in the class.

MINDFULNESS IN AN INNER-CITY HIGH SCHOOL

Here is one example of mindfulness implemented in a high school in the Bronx, one of the poorest inner-city districts in New York City (Davis, 2015). Within many inner-city schools, students exposed to trauma are somewhat more common than in other schools because of the increased poverty, food insecurity, and crime found in some inner-city communities. Once implemented at this Bronx school, mindfulness was embraced by students and teachers alike.

Vignette 6.1 Mindfulness in the classroom

Argos Gonzalez taught an English class with a mix of African American and Hispanic students. When the class began, Mr. Gonzalez rang a bell and said, "Today we're going to talk about mindfulness. You guys remember what mindfulness is?" When no

(Continued)

Vignette 6.1 (Continued)

one spoke, Mr. Gonzalez gestured to one of the posters displayed in the classroom that summarized an earlier lesson on mindfulness. In that lesson, the students had brainstormed the meaning of mindfulness and listed some phrases such as "being focused," "being aware of my surroundings," and "being aware of my feelings."

Mr. Gonzalez continued with the following instructions: "I'm going to say a couple of words to you about emotions. You're not literally going to feel these emotions, but each word is going to trigger something; it's going to make you think of something or feel something. Try to explore it. First, sit up straight, and put your feet flat on the ground. Let your eyes close."

Mr. Gonzalez tapped the bell again, as a signal for the class to become quiet. Then he said, "Take a deep breath into your belly. As you breathe in and breathe out, notice that your breath is going to be stronger in a certain part of your body. Maybe it's your belly, your chest, or your nose. We'll begin by counting to 10 breaths. Then I'll say a couple words about emotions, and you focus only on the one thought that comes to your mind. If you get lost in thought, it's okay. Just come back to your one thought. Whether you get up to 10 or not doesn't really matter. It's just a way to focus your mind." Then the students practiced that mindfulness activity for several minutes (Davis, 2015).

Teachers around the world, like Mr. Gonzalez, are choosing to spend 10–15 minutes of precious class time daily on this type of procedure for one simple reason: Mindfulness strengthens students' learning and self-control to a point where less time is taken to conduct the mindfulness exercises than would be expended on managing students' behavior problems were the mindfulness program not in place. Teachers would not continue to invest this time unless the benefits were clearly evident in their own classrooms (Davis, 2015), and in an inner-city school, this type of stress reduction intervention can be life-changing for some students.

In fact, teachers using mindfulness constantly report increased productivity and fewer behavior problems among their students, and a better class climate overall, when they teach the students mindfulness (Albrecht et al., 2012; Greenberg & Harris, 2012; Harris, 2015). Today, schools all across the United States and the United Kingdom are beginning to practice mindfulness daily in the classroom (Davis, 2015) because these benefits among all students are so apparent, and the mood regulation mindfulness fosters is particularly important for children exposed to trauma.

On rare occasions, some parents might express concern about mindfulness instruction if the yoga aspect is overly emphasized. However, by approaching mindfulness with a focus on quieting the mind to empower children to reduce stress, depression, and anxiety and improving student well-being, teachers can usually forestall any potential parental concern of this nature. Of course, parents should be fully informed of how this practice will be taught and should also be assured that no overt religious training is taking place (Welham, 2014).

IMPLEMENTING MINDFULNESS

In addition to the published curricula, there are many individually developed approaches to teaching mindfulness in medical, therapeutic, and classroom settings, and various approaches stress different things. These range from intentional breathing while seated to walking meditations (Ackerman, 2018; Welham, 2014). The suggested procedures that follow come from a variety of sources (Ackerman, 2018; Caprino, 2014; Davis, 2015; Quirk, 2023; Welham, 2014) and represent the types of mindfulness exercises being done in schools. Further, this strategy can be implemented by teachers, clinicians, and parents alike based on the information herein, coupled with the examples found on YouTube. Here are some mindfulness activities to do daily for 5–10 minutes. Once a teacher selects one of these activities, the class should do that same one for a period of at least two weeks prior to using another idea so the students grow accustomed to the practice.

Breathing Exercises

Breathing exercises were discussed in Vignette 6.1, when Mr. Gonzalez had students count their breaths in a calm, soothing setting. Today, many teachers teach breathing exercises to focus students' attention and help them relax (Ackerman, 2018). Such relaxation will help reduce stress and even foster higher student engagement in subsequent academic periods.

Self-Regulation Through Mood/Emotional Awareness

As discussed in Chapter 2, teachers in trauma-informed schools generally teach students a bit about the human brain and regions of the brain associated with different types of moods and thought processes (e.g., the amygdala as the emotional brain and the neocortex as the planning brain or "smart part"). Students learn a bit about how their brains function, and then they can refer to those brain regions while they explore their own moods and behaviors, or the moods and behaviors of others (Welham, 2014).

Over time, even students who have undergone significant long-term trauma can learn to exert influence on their own moods and emotions, and such self-regulation will help them achieve more balance in their lives overall. Several other examples such as the mood wheel and the anger thermometer, both described in Chapter 5, are activities that can help students develop awareness and control over their moods. Still, as in the previous example, mindfulness specifically teaches students to "control" their thoughts (e.g., by focusing on only one thing or counting breaths), and such specific instruction in self-regulation is critical for students exposed to trauma.

Senses and Sensory Awareness

Some mindfulness trainers have students practice attention skills by stressing sensory stimuli. Students might be asked to chew a raisin (only one raisin) for an entire minute—chewing slowly and focusing their attention only on the sensation of chewing or how the raisin tastes. Alternatively, students might touch different-textured clothes while they concentrate on the sensations with their eyes closed. Again, this focused thought strengthens students' ability to self-regulate their emotions.

Focused Awareness Activities

Focused awareness involves having students focus on something other than sensory experiences, while stressing that students do only one thing at a time (e.g., walking, looking at nature, or completing a morning reading with no distractions or outside thoughts allowed). This will help students develop task persistence and focused attention (Ackerman, 2018).

Daily Quiet Time or Visualization

Quiet time and *three-minute meditation time* are terms used by schools to emphasize how students can choose to become focused on a quiet, peaceful image, perhaps a picture of a mountain stream or visualization of the ocean shore (Oaklander, 2015; Schwartz, 2016). Several videos listed on the companion website show the use of quiet time. Some teachers use a small bell as a signal for meditation or quiet time to begin and end. Once students have been shown what to do during quiet time, they generally go immediately into meditation for a two- or three-minute period at the sound of the bell, and then they come back more focused and ready to work (Davis, 2015).

THE TURTLE TECHNIQUE: A RELAXATION STRATEGY

While mindfulness may be used with students as young as the primary grades (Ackerman, 2018), well before that idea was developed other relaxation strategies were used with very young children. As early as the 1970s, various researchers saw a need for teaching young students who were prone to aggression and violence in schools a relatively simple way to un-stress or de-escalate potentially violent emotions. Marlene Schneider and associates (Robin, Schneider, & Dolnick, 1976; Schneider, 1974) developed the Turtle Technique, a self-regulation technique that consists of three components: the turtle relaxation phase, a problem-solving phase, and peer support.

The image of a turtle withdrawing into its shell is explained as a protective space from which the turtle can stop interacting with the external environment. Young children are taught to "withdraw into their shells" by placing their heads on their desks, locking their arms under their heads, and closing their eyes (Robin et al., 1976). They are told that this is how the turtle protects itself from the outside world. While in the turtle position, children are taught to relax their muscles and ignore any sounds in the class while they begin to cope with any emotional tensions.

After a period of relaxation in the turtle position, the students might be asked to discuss with the teacher what happened and/or begin a series of problem-solving activities that allow them to reflect on a stressful event in class or on their behavior (Robin et al., 1976). Once they know the technique, young students are expected to "do a turtle" when they are feeling fear, rage, or anger. Also, teachers can request that a student do a turtle when they perceive that the child is moving into a dysregulated state.

Beyond teaching the turtle response itself, two additional aspects of this technique should be emphasized. First, after the turtle relaxation, students engage in some reflective problem solving concerning their behavior (Fleming,

Ritchie, & Fleming, 1983; Robin et al., 1976). For example, in the study by Fleming and colleagues (1983), four basic problem-solving steps were taught to the students: (1) identify the problem, (2) generate alternative solutions, (3) evaluate alternatives and select the most appropriate, and (4) implement the selected alternative. In that study, students first did a turtle relaxation for a 10- to 15-minute period, and then answered those questions in a discussion with the teacher.

Second, it is critical that the other members of the class respect the student's choice to become a "turtle" for a few minutes. Thus, the Turtle Technique should be taught to all class members together, with the emphasis that, "when someone is in the turtle position, everybody else leaves them alone!" The class should be instructed not to talk to, joke with, or talk about students who have chosen to withdraw into their shell.

The same idea, without the turtle example, can be used with students up through Grade 12. While use of the turtle metaphor itself should probably be limited to Grades K–4, older students may be taught the same relaxation technique by calling it a time-out. For example, students in secondary school might be encouraged to signal the teacher that they need a time-out using the same time-out signal used in football. The student could then place their head on their desk for a one- or two-minute time-out and momentarily escape from the social demands of the classroom. Both teachers and students should agree not to call on or ask questions of students while they are in this time-out period. Then the student in time-out might be asked to write down brief answers to the four self-reflection questions, and the teacher could have a follow-up discussion with the child at the end of class.

RESEARCH ON MINDFULNESS AND RELAXATION TRAINING

Mindfulness and other relaxation ideas have received general research support in both the classroom and clinical settings (Ackerman, 2018; Albrecht et al., 2012; Campbell, 2013; Felver et al., 2022; Greenberg & Harris, 2012; Klatta et al., 2013; Quirk, 2023; Robin et al., 1976; Schneider, 1974; Schonert-Reichl & Lawlor, 2010; Schwartz, 2016; Semple et al., 2005; Thomas, 2016). These studies indicate a number of positive benefits of mindfulness programs in schools, including reduced stress; improved regulation of one's own moods; improved capacity for compassion and empathy; decreased anxiety, depression, and aggression in the classroom; and increased attention. Further, several studies have reported improved classroom behavior and even increased academic scores resulting from mindfulness training (Ackerman, 2018; Albrecht et al., 2012; Oaklander, 2015). Clearly, this body of research demonstrates the potential of using mindfulness or relaxation practices for students exposed to trauma, as well as students with attention deficit hyperactivity disorder, aggression, mood disorders, and other mental health diagnoses.

One example of classroom-based action research on mindfulness was presented by Schwartz (2016). After implementation of daily mindfulness activities for a period of weeks at a K–8 school in Portland, Oregon, both teachers and students demonstrated clear benefits from mindfulness training. Data showed that office disciplinary referrals were decreased and that both teachers and students reported a drastically improved school climate as a result of the mindfulness program. In short, this and other research (Ackerman, 2018; Felver et al., 2022) support the idea that mindfulness is an effective strategy to reduce depression, stress, aggression, and anxiety while improving mood and emotional self-regulation, attention skills, behavior, and social skills.

A CASE STUDY ON MINDFULNESS

Mr. Trenton had two students in his fourth-grade class who had suffered abuse as young children, and both were constantly disturbing the class with aggressive disciplinary outbursts, either verbal or physical. He had to stop class almost daily to deal with aggression from one, if not both, of these students. Mr. Trenton determined to try a mindfulness approach by using a daily "quiet reflection time." First, he gathered baseline data showing the number of aggressive or other behavioral problems of the two students (Mike and Darius) over a one-week period as shown in Figure 6.1.

These data show that during the first week, both Mike and Darius disrupted the class several times each day, so some intervention was necessary for each student. To do this intervention, Mr. Trenton began a "training week" during which he taught various mindfulness exercises to his entire class, with each 10-minute training session followed by a three-minute meditation period. During the training sessions, Mr. Trenton talked with the children about different feelings, such as anger, frustration, depression, fear, happiness, joy, and so forth, and he illustrated each mood or emotion with a "face" picture showing the emotion or mood discussed. He urged the class to ask themselves, "How am I feeling?" and then indicate the face that most closely represented their feeling. This was intended to help students become aware of their feelings. Then, each

Figure 6.1 • *Disruptive behaviors data for Mike and Darius*

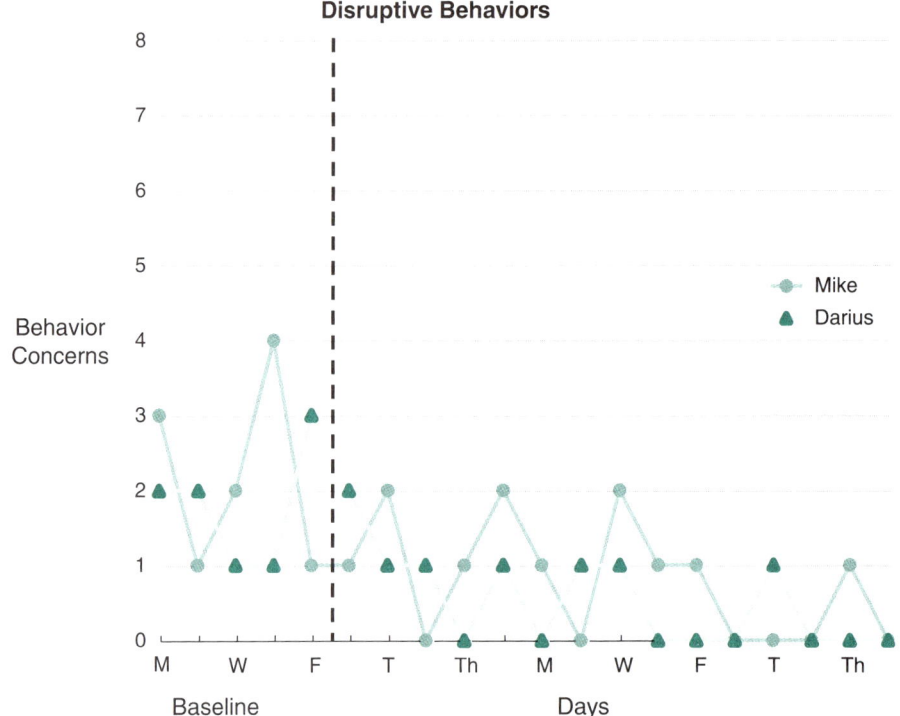

day, he urged students to do a "mindful moment," a quiet-time meditation similar to the breathing exercise Mr. Gonzalez used in Vignette 6.1

 https://bit.ly/3T9YEVH

(see the QR code provided on this page for an example of a mindful moment). As in that class, Mr. Trenton tapped the edge of a metal bowl to make a ring sound to signal the beginning and end of the three-minute meditation.

During the training week and for two weeks thereafter, Mr. Trenton continued to keep a chart of misbehaviors of both Darius and Mike. As the data show, the misbehaviors of these two students began to decline as soon as the training began and were reduced significantly by the end of the in-class, action research project. Total misbehaviors were reduced from an average of 4.0 daily (between the two students) to 0.4 daily by the last week of the intervention. These data show how mindfulness exercises can work to reduce misbehavior over time. At the urging of his principal, Mr. Trenton then shared these data during the next faculty meeting.

For students exposed to trauma, these types of data speak volumes when shared with school counselors and parents. Therefore, we encourage all teachers using this strategy to keep a data chart by simply counting the behavioral problems before starting the intervention and for several weeks thereafter. Such data should be shared with everyone, including students, to emphasize that they have learned to control their moods and behaviors.

SUMMARY

Research demonstrates that mindfulness should be considered for implementation in practically all grade levels for most children in schools, including students exposed to trauma (Ackerman, 2018; Felver et al., 2022). From the primary grades through high school, this instructional strategy improves class behavior and performance for many students exposed to trauma, as well as students exhibiting other behavior problems, so much so that teachers are making time for mindfulness exercises and have repeatedly asserted that this is time well spent (Davis, 2015; Schwartz, 2016). Further, all children and teens seem to benefit from mindfulness and/or other relaxation training in terms of stress reduction and self-regulation of moods and emotions. In short, this will be time well spent for all students in the class, and it may help save a child exposed to trauma from severe depression, consistent anger, or suicide.

REFERENCES

Ackerman, C. E. (2018, June 27). *The why and how of mindfulness in schools (+31 teaching tips)*. Retrieved from https://positivepsychology.com/mindfulness-education/

Albrecht, N. J., Albrecht, P. M., & Cohen, M. (2012). Mindfully teaching in the classroom: A literature review. *Australian Journal of Teacher Education, 37*(12), 1–13.

Campbell, E. (2013, October 10). Research round-up: Mindfulness in schools. *Greater Good*. Retrieved from https://greatergood.berkeley.edu/article/item/research_round_up_school_based_mindfulness_programs

Caprino, K. (2014, February 12). 5 mindfulness steps that guarantee increased success and vitality. *Forbes*. Retrieved from http:/www.forbes.com/sites/kathycaprino/2014/02/12/5-mindfulness-steps-that-guarantee-increased-success-and-vitality

Davis, L. C. (2015, August 31). When mindfulness meets the classroom. *The Atlantic*. Retrieved from https://theatlanti.com/education/archive/2015/08/mindfulness-education-schools-mediation/402469/

Felver, J. C., Clawson, A. J., Ash, T. L., Martens, B. K., Wang, Q., & Singh, N. N. (2022). Meta-analysis of mindfulness-based program Soles of the Feet for disruptive behaviors. *Behavior Modification*, *46*(6), 1488–1516.

Fleming, D. C., Ritchie, B., & Fleming, E. R. (1983). Fostering the social adjustment of disturbed students. *Teaching Exceptional Children*, 15, 172–175.

Greenberg, M. T., & Harris, A. R. (2012). Nurturing mindfulness in children and youth: Current state of research. *Child Development Perspectives*, *6*(2), 161–166.

Harris, E. A. (2015, October 24). Under stress: Students in New York schools find calm in meditation. *The New York Times*. Retrieved from https://www.nytimes.com/2015/10/24/nyregion/under-stress-students-in-new-york-schools-find-calm-in-meditation.html

Klatta, M., Harpsterb, K., Brownea, E., White, S., & Case-Smith, J. (2013). Feasibility and preliminary outcomes for Move-Into-Learning: An arts-based mindfulness classroom intervention. *Journal of Positive Psychology*, *8*(3), 233–241. Retrieved from https://www.tandfonline.com/doi/abs/10.1080/17439760.2013.779011

Oaklander, M. (2015, February 5). A nation of mini-meditators. *Time*. Retrieved from https://time.com/3696861/a-nation-of-mini-meditators/

Quirk, M. (2023, February 9). The benefits of mindfulness education in schools. *Psychology Today*. Retrieved from https://www.psychologytoday.com/us/blog/evidence-based-living/202302/the-benefits-of-mindfulness-education-in-schools

Robin, A., Schneider, M., & Dolnick, M. (1976). The Turtle Technique: An extended case study of self-control in the classroom. *Psychology in the Schools*, *13*, 448–453.

Schneider, M. (1974). Turtle Technique in the classroom. *Teaching Exceptional Children*, 7, 21–24.

Schonert-Reichl, K. A., & Lawlor, M. S. (2010). The effects of a mindfulness-based education program on pre- and early adolescents' well-being and social and emotional competence. *Mindfulness*, *1*, 137–151.

Schwartz, K. (2016, March 30). *What changes when a school embraces mindfulness?* KQED. Retrieved from https://www.kqed.org/mindshift/44405/what-changes-when-a-school-embraces-mindfulness

Semple, R. J., Reid, E. F. G., & Miller, L. (2005). Treating anxiety with mindfulness: An open trial of mindfulness training for anxious children. *Journal of Cognitive Psychotherapy, 19*(4), 379–392.

Thomas, L. (2016, February 1). Mindful facilitation: Don't do something, Just stand there. *Edutopia*. Retrieved from https://www.edutopia.org/blog/mindful-facilitation-pbl-laura-thomas

Welham, H. (2014, July 23). How to introduce mindfulness into your classroom: Nine handy tips. *The Guardian*. Retrieved from https:www.theguardian.com/teacher-network/teacher-blog/2014/jul/23/how-to-mindfulness-classroom-tips

CHAPTER 7

JOURNALING FOR STUDENTS EXPOSED TO TRAUMA

Journaling interventions involve having students write about their experiences, emotions, and moods, or events in their private life, by making entries in a personal journal (Scott, 2023; Tartakovsky, 2022; University of Rochester Medical Center, 2024; WebMD, 2021). Journaling in the school context usually involves a regularly scheduled time, daily or biweekly, during which students write in their journals. The journal entries are then, at various times, reviewed by the teacher (Adams, 2023). Teachers and students may choose to discuss journal entries on a scheduled basis or simply as necessary. The purpose is generally to empower the students to consider their emotions and moods in a more concrete manner, and thus establish some control over them (Tartakovsky, 2022).

Like many other strategies described in this book, journaling can be widely used in schools, in counseling sessions, or by parents. Children as young as five can "write" in journals via drawing pictures, or by selecting from emojis provided by their teachers and copying those into their journals. These variations make journaling applicable and effective across a wider age range (Krentzman, Hoeppner, Hoeppner, & Barnett, 2022; Lewis, 2017; Scott, 2023). Further, this is a "low cost" strategy; monetary costs only involve the purchase of a notebook or journal itself, and the cost of time is fairly minimal—perhaps 10–15 minutes daily, or twice a week. Of course, should a teacher or counselor choose to talk with a student about a particular journal entry, that will take some additional time outside of class, but such a discussion is not necessary for every journal entry.

For reaching students severely affected by trauma (who, as noted previously, are at times seemingly difficult to engage), a journal can be the perfect self-reflection tool, and follow-up discussions with the teacher or counselor can become an important outlet for students' emotions. Further, this use of student journaling fosters and encourages some trust between the professional and the student, which, as previously discussed, can be a significant challenge when working with students exposed to trauma.

VARIOUS TYPES OF JOURNALS

Many types of journaling are used in schools today (Tartakovsky, 2022), though open-topic, expressive journaling is probably the most common form. In this type of journal, students are expected to write down their feelings, thoughts, or examples of situations that made them feel proud, fearful, uncomfortable, or another emotion during the day. They essentially write freely about any topic they choose. Usually, a 10- to 15-minute period during class is provided for making these journal entries, and other than the general suggestion to "write about your emotions or feelings," no direction is given as to what topics to cover. Students may write or draw in their journals on anything from a TikTok video to an altercation that they may have witnessed at school. These entries then provide a teacher or counselor with a possible topic for discussion with the child. For teachers serving kids exposed to trauma, open-ended journaling options are probably the best choice because these journal assignments offer students unlimited opportunity to communicate about their thoughts and feelings without having to concentrate on only one topic.

In contrast to expressive journaling, some teachers and clinicians use more focused journaling, where a specific focus or topic is suggested for journal entries (Tartakovsky, 2022). For example, mathematics teachers may require students to journal about specific topics in math to help combat students' anxieties about the subject matter. Students in other classes may be journaling about poetry or literature by noting specific themes common to several writings.

Other students may be told to write a gratitude journal, in which they list and discuss all the things that they are thankful for each day. For students exposed to trauma, this may help them focus on positive things in life and can provide a description of daily events that can be referred to during troubled times in the future. Teachers or clinicians may remind them to look back at their gratitude journal when these kids are feeling down. Further, when these students are unhappy, teachers can request that they focus on something positive by writing in the gratitude journal, thus reinforcing the idea that children can self-regulate their emotions and moods to some degree.

Alternatively, an "anger journal" may be used to help students explore their feelings of anger or frustration and, over time, to develop more positive reflections about and responses to their anger. For some students exposed to trauma, an anger journal may be the tactic that allows them to gain some control over their anger, as well as the behaviors they engage in while angry. An example of Dr. Bender using an anger journal is presented on the companion website for this book (https://traumahelpnow.com).

As this discussion shows, many types of focused journaling options exist, and additional options from a variety of sources are presented in Box 7.1 (Adams, 2023; Scott, 2023; Tartakovsky, 2022). We generally recommend that teachers use a variety of these ideas for the journal assignments, and perhaps vary the assignments from week to week to keep them interesting for the students.

Box 7.1 Types of focused journals

- **Emotional release:** In this type of journal, students write about things that were stressful, emotional, or even particularly enjoyable during the day. While these entries can focus on both positive and negative emotional events, the ratio of positive to negative is important to consider for stress reduction. The more positive things included in the journal, compared to negative things, the more positive students may feel overall. Teachers should discuss that ratio with the students, pointing out the benefits of positive journaling in terms of stress reduction (Scott, 2023).
- **Bullet journal:** This is a personal planning journal that lists, in bullet form, the types of activities that a student must accomplish. For many individuals, being more organized in this fashion helps alleviate stress.
- **Sentence stems:** Sentence stems have long been used by teachers as a way to help reluctant writers write, and one or more such stems can help students in journaling. Stems such as "Right now I feel…" or "Today I was most happy when…" can help students get their feelings out (Adams, 2023).
- **Areas-of-life inventory:** An inventory of various areas of life can focus students on what's going on in their lives. This technique may include stems such as "At school today, the most important thing was…" or "At home yesterday…" or "My feelings today were generally very…" Other areas to inventory may involve work, spirituality, health, or family.
- **Clustering my feelings/thoughts:** This type of journal entry or technique involves both writing and artistic creation—briefly writing down words or

(Continued)

(Continued)

thoughts, then drawing connecting lines to show relationships. Students can focus on a core thought, issue, event, or problem and then make connections with specific times or events during the day.

- **Listing:** Journaling can begin with listing ideas such as "Five things I enjoyed today were…" or "Today my five biggest worries were…"
- **Captured moments:** This type of journal entry will focus on writing a brief vignette about a daily event. Ideas include "My best time today was…" or "My happiest moment happened when…"
- **Unsent letters:** Students can be told to imagine a positive or negative thing they might wish to say to someone. Whereas sharing positive ideas or thoughts is always advisable, sometimes sharing negative thoughts can help students clarify their thinking. This is the advantage of having students write a letter that they will not send. Point out to the students that this writing process can help them understand their thoughts but that it is wise to not actually send such letters.

HOW TO BEGIN JOURNALING

A variety of authors have provided suggestions for getting started in journaling (Greenwald, 2020; Grothaus, 2015; Lewis, 2017; Scott, 2023; Tartakovsky, 2022; University of Rochester Medical Center, 2024). Generally, the only things students need to begin journaling are a pen and a notebook; any type of notebook will do for a journal. Alternatively, many teachers encourage journaling on the computer, thus resulting in a digital file of journal entries (Grothaus, 2015). For younger students, providing pictures of emojis representing common emotions (joy, anger, sadness, etc.) on the classroom walls and letting students copy those emojis into their journals can help them begin journaling. Teachers and clinicians have also provided stickers that represent the various emotions, which allows younger students to put them directly into the journal.

Next, teachers should determine what types of time might be devoted to journaling, when it should take place, and how students should do their journaling (Adams, 2023; Scott, 2023; Tartakovsky, 2022). Sometimes teachers and clinicians use the "story starter" idea to help older students begin their writing. While merely making paper, pen, and writing time available to kids in the classroom can work for some students, providing a sentence stem or beginning question on a topic may help more reluctant students to begin the journal writing process. As one might guess, for many students who have experienced some failure in school, a blank page can be quite intimidating. Thus, having some structuring questions to assist in journaling can be helpful. Typically, providing a few simple, guiding questions seems to work best as it provides some guidance but does not restrict topics available to the student.

In anger journals, as one example, a set of guided questions can help students focus on how to effectively manage their emotions and actions while feeling anger. For an anger journal, we recommend the following questions:

1. *What made me angry, and what did I do?*
2. *What happened as a result of my actions?*
3. *Could I have managed my angry feelings better to get a different outcome?*

Another issue to consider involves the openness or level of privacy of the journal entries. The topic of privacy in journal entries should be discussed with children above a certain age, typically around Grade 3 and higher. Generally, teachers and clinicians should assure students that the journal entries will remain private, and that other students will not be allowed to see these private journal entries unless the student wants them to be shared in class. However, honesty is the key to the trust that students affected by trauma need to develop with the teacher or counselor, so these professionals must explain confidentiality to the students in an age-appropriate manner. It is important for even younger students to understand that, on occasion, their parents or the school counselor may review some journal entries, if the teacher thinks that is necessary.

Also, in the upper grades, students should be told that journal entries may be shared if they present a dangerous situation impacting a student's safety. This is required by law in most states. Of course, for students who may be victimized by parents or others at home, this lack of total privacy may impact what the student chooses to share in the journal. However, there are instances in which various types of traumas in a child's life have come to light based on journal entries, so we encourage teachers to have this discussion about the limited privacy of journal entries with the students in an age-appropriate fashion.

Additional guidelines and tips for journaling have been provided in the literature to help teachers get started in the journaling process (Adams, 2023; Grothaus, 2015; Lewis, 2017; Scott, 2023; University of Rochester Medical Center, 2024). These are presented in Box 7.2.

Box 7.2 Additional guidelines for journaling

- **Have students write every day if possible:** Journaling can become quite engaging, so teachers should limit the time students have for journaling. Most teachers generally recommend between 10 and 20 minutes daily.
- **Have students keep it simple:** Students might keep a pen and paper handy at all times so that when they want to jot down thoughts, they can. Some students carry a small writing pad along with them all the time, and such journaling should be encouraged, even after school.
- **Pick a writing medium that works in your class:** Some argue that pen and paper are the best media for journaling, since these can go anywhere and there is evidence that the writing process with pen and paper stimulates certain brain regions more than working on a computer (Grothaus, 2015). Others suggest that journaling on a computer is best. We suggest that teachers pick a medium that works in their classroom and stick with it. Teachers might wish to try a combination, asking students to keep journal ideas on paper in their pocket, and later express them more fully in a computer file.
- **Have students write whatever feels right:** Ultimately, this is their journal, and students should not have to worry about any particular structure, unless a structure is recommended to focus the class on one issue or to help students who are reluctant writers.
- **Do not edit or grade journal entries:** Journaling should be an occasion for the free flow of ideas, and words should flow freely from one's heart without worrying about spelling mistakes or what other people might think. Only students and teachers will see the journals, and while the teacher's natural inclination is to "correct" the journal, this is strongly discouraged because, at least for kids exposed to trauma, teachers typically use journals as an open communication tool.
- **Share journal entries as the student wishes:** Students might choose to share their journal with close friends, but they should be cautioned to remember that journals contain some of their deepest thoughts, and it is up to them whether they share with other students.
- **Journal in the same place daily:** For in-class journaling, have students pick a spot in the classroom (e.g., their desk, a comfortable rug, floor space) to journal in daily. Getting students away from their desks, if other comfortable seating options are available, can facilitate the journaling process.
- **Require a table of contents:** Tables of contents can help students with long-term reflection on a given problem, particularly if they can find previous journal entries from weeks or months ago on the same issue. The table of

contents will help in that process. Generally, students should add a few items to the table of contents every four or five days.

- **Write teacher comments:** While not all journal entries will be reviewed by the teacher all the time, when teachers do review journal entries, they should make brief comments to encourage the students or ask questions about these entries. Likewise, some teachers encourage students to highlight or specifically identify any journal entries they want the teacher to read.

BENEFITS OF JOURNALING FOR STUDENTS EXPOSED TO TRAUMA

Journaling holds many benefits for students exposed to adverse childhood experiences, or ACEs (Adams, 2023; Tartakovsky, 2022; WebMD, 2021). During the journaling process, it is not uncommon that deeply reflective and emotional thoughts emerge in the journal pages, and thus journals allow these students one opportunity to share their feelings and their deepest thoughts about the challenges within their lives. This is why clinicians often include journaling in therapeutic treatment plans for both children and adults with various mental health diagnoses. Further, various sources have identified an array of other benefits of journaling for mental health, as presented in Box 7.3 (Lewis, 2017; Scott, 2023; Sohal, Singh, Dhillon, & Gill, 2022; Ullrich & Lutgendorf, 2002; University of Rochester Medical Center, 2024; WebMD, 2021).

Box 7.3 Other health benefits of journaling

- Manage anxiety
- Improve mobility among arthritis patients
- Cope with depression
- Help wounds heal faster
- Control stress-related symptoms
- Understand and improve one's moods
- Decrease symptoms of asthma and arthritis
- Prioritize problems and fears
- Control triggers for depression and anxiety
- Identify negative thoughts and behaviors
- Provide an opportunity for positive self-talk
- Decrease blood pressure
- Develop a plan to resolve problems

In addition to mental health benefits, there are measurable, documented medical benefits associated with journaling. Not only does journaling reduce stress overall; it also improves immune system functioning at the biochemical level in the body (Fritson, 2008; Grothaus, 2015; Scott, 2023). This physical result of journaling indicates the potential strength and importance of this strategy for kids exposed to trauma who have survived harsh challenges during their childhood. If physiological changes such as these result from journaling, it is easy to see that positive psychological changes such as stress reduction and increased relaxation can likewise result, and the research, reviewed briefly later in this chapter, has consistently shown these benefits of journaling.

Further, because both trust and control are huge issues among children and adolescents challenged by trauma, finding methods to foster trust by encouraging students to share their thoughts, feelings, and fears is critical. As the journaling process proceeds, most students begin to sense that they have some degree of control over their moods and emotions. In expressive-writing journal assignments, any topic can be acceptable for the journal since the student controls what is written down and what is not. Thus, the students can choose to trust the teacher or clinician as much or as little as they wish. Once some level of trust is established between the student and the professional, the journal can serve as a critically important communication mechanism for students exposed to trauma.

Next, some students who might be embarrassed to share their experiences when directly talking with their teachers or counselors may find that they can share those feelings more easily by writing them down in a journal entry, even knowing that the teacher will be reading the journal at a later time. In short, journaling tends to develop a trusting relationship between teacher and student, which is highly desirable for these students.

Finally, many students impacted by trauma encounter academic difficulties in the classroom. However, limited writing ability does not prohibit the use of journaling for any child as accommodations can be provided. Talk-to-text software programs are available on most computers, and many smartphones today allow students to journal by merely speaking. This can extend the benefits of journaling into much lower grade levels, as well as to students with academic delay in writing. Thus, journaling is strongly recommended for virtually all kids challenged by trauma, from kindergarten through Grade 12.

GROUP JOURNAL WRITING

Most teachers and clinicians implement journal writing as an individual task because the intent in journaling is to provide students with opportunities to share their deeper thoughts, emotions, and concerns. However, sometimes shared journaling or partner writing journal activities can be of particular benefit for students exposed to trauma, specifically to help these students develop more trusting personal relationships (Adams, 2023). Working in groups of two or three, students might be required to jointly write a shared journal, or to write in each other's journals on a topic specified by one student or another. As you might imagine, this can help shy or reluctant students participate more in the journal writing process since the social expectation in a shared journal writing assignment can motivate some students.

This type of shared experience in journaling is particularly useful in academic journaling. For example, two or three students might be asked to journal about shared anxiety relative to their mathematics or science homework. These shared writing experiences often let students understand that they are not alone in their academic anxieties and may promote higher participation and sharing of ideas. Creative teachers might even find ways to use social-networking platforms such as X (formerly Twitter) for this type of assignment, thus making group journaling particularly appealing to today's digital learners. Also, in some highly digital classes, a classwide chat room or discussion board may be used for this shared writing process. Adams (2023) provides a series of other ideas for journal writing that can be the basis for shared journal writing activities, and these are presented in Box 7.4.

Box 7.4 Group journal writing

- **Alphabet lines.** Teachers begin this type of journaling by writing the alphabet from *A* to *Z* vertically down the side of a page. Students should then be encouraged to write a poem or story in which each successive line begins with the next letter.
- **Dialog:** Two or three students might be encouraged to write an imaginary dialog on a particular problem or situation. One student can suggest a topic or problem, and others may be encouraged to write from differing perspectives about the topic.
- **Character sketch:** Developing a character sketch in journaling is similar to describing a character in a story. Working together, students might be required to add to the character description based on their own experiences.

CAUTIONS IN JOURNALING

Research does raise several cautions in using journaling in relation to a trauma-informed classroom. Most of these questions deal with the time it takes to write or review journals, maximizing the positive impact of journaling, and managing dangerous or destructive issues that arise in journaling (Finley, 2010; Lewis, 2017; Stosny, 2013). In short, journaling can either help or hurt, depending on how this teaching approach is used (Stosny, 2013). Here are some suggestions to assist in these areas of caution.

Time Management for Journaling

Finding time to have students write in their journals can be a challenge (Adams, 2023; Greenwald, 2020; Tartakovsky, 2022). Of course, the benefits of journaling are most readily realized when teachers make the time to allow students to write in their journals more frequently, so many elementary teachers find some time for daily writing (Lewis, 2017). For teachers who are concerned with time and are new to journaling, journal assignments can be given once or twice a week initially. Also, if pen and paper are the journal medium of choice, students can be encouraged to do additional journaling at home or whenever they feel like it. Some students fall in love with journaling and continue to do this long after class or the academic year ends.

While reserving some time for daily journaling in the elementary classroom seems possible to many teachers, this issue is more pressing in departmentalized schools since it is hard to find journaling time within a daily 55-minute algebra period, as one example. With that noted, topical academic journals may still be used in those departmentalized classes, and students can be encouraged to do journaling once or twice a week at the end of class, or as a homework activity.

A more serious issue is how the teacher finds time to review journal entries. Psychologists and counselors typically review almost all journal entries. However, in most instances, teachers cannot review all journal entries for all students due to time constraints.

Of course, many of the benefits of journaling will not be realized unless the teacher makes time to reflectively review at least some of the journal entries on a regular basis, but every teacher's time is quite limited. We can almost hear our readers asking, "Who has that kind of time to review journals?"

However, in considering the reality of teaching kids exposed to trauma, we would like to suggest turning that question around: "Who can afford not to do journaling?" (Finley, 2010; Lewis, 2017). We have been in our own classrooms, and we understand the time constraints of teachers, but we also know that journaling has many benefits for these kids and may, on occasion, help free children from dangerous situations. Further, as trust develops between the teacher or clinician and the students, journaling is quite likely to alleviate some of the extreme behavior problems commonly demonstrated by students impacted by trauma in the classroom. In some cases, it is possible that this activity actually saves teachers time, since prohibiting those misbehaviors via journaling may ultimately take less time than managing them once they occur. If some mechanism for sharing their deep thoughts and feelings is not provided to these students, all veteran teachers can easily imagine the time they will have to spend in extreme disciplinary efforts for these kids exposed to trauma! In short, isn't a journaling assignment, which can be done by all kids in the class, more beneficial than time spent responding to disciplinary problems for one or a few kids? In that context, teachers will quickly see the benefits of journaling assignments for students exposed to trauma as well as others in the class.

With that thought noted, reviewing some journal entries for all students is important, as such review stresses the importance of journaling. Teachers should always write a note or two in students' journals to let the kids know their journal entries were read even when a teacher–child discussion is not necessary. Also, teachers should discuss some journal entries with every student, as time allows. Teachers can also invite the students to let the teacher know when to review a particular journal entry, and this idea tends to increase trust and communication with the students. When used in that manner, journals can become a relatively private and protected mechanism for communication between the teacher and the student who has been exposed to trauma.

Maximizing the Positive Impact of Journaling

For some students who undergo severe trauma challenges in their home life, journals can become focused almost exclusively on negative events or challenging life circumstances, and thus journaling might have the negative effect of seemingly reinforcing how horrible life can be (Stosny, 2013). To prevent this outcome, teachers should always encourage children to focus on some positive events, feelings, or experiences in their journal entries, along with teasing out the negative events or problematic situations. Further, even for negative events or emotions, having the students use their journal entries both to describe their thoughts and emotions and then to seek and identify some possible resolutions to the problem can transform even the most negative journal entries into important learning opportunities.

Some research has shown that journals can do harm to students if the activity seems to emphasize the idea that students are merely passive observers of horrible situations in life. Clearly, journals should not become vehicles of blame or merely list all the negative things in a child's life. To alleviate this problem, should it arise, Stosny (2013) urges teachers to make journaling a more positive experience by going further than merely describing negative events. Students should be encouraged to reflect on and evaluate their emotions as they explore solutions to various problems and issues. Students may also be encouraged to "convert negative energy into positive energy" by finding alternatives for how they might behave the next time a negative situation arises.

When used in this fashion, journaling can help students lower their emotional reactivity to negative situations, and perhaps consider positive courses of action for similar tough situations. Stosny (2013) provides a series of questions that teachers might use to help students develop positive journal entries and/or to positively reflect on negative events or feelings that come to light in journaling. These are presented in Box 7.5.

Box 7.5 Developing positive journal entries

- Write a few sentences about a problem, event, situation, or negative feeling that you have had. Try to look objectively at the thoughts, emotions, and behaviors you expressed. Would you think the same if you felt comfortable? Can you convert the negative energy into positive creativity and growth?
- Are you acting according to your deepest values and the kind of person you want to be?
- How are your actions in this experience in keeping with your deepest values? Would you feel the same if you were firmly in touch with your core values?
- Write a few sentences considering each of the following: What can you learn from this matter? Can you grow from this experience? How can what you learn make the world a better place and you a better person? Can you tolerate a certain amount of ambiguity or lack of clarity about this matter? Is it okay to have mixed feelings about the matter you described?
- Can you raise your confidence to deal with the worst-case scenario should it occur? Do you have a plan of action should the worst-case scenario happen?

- What are the perspectives of other people in your problem description? How would they describe the events? What core hurts might they be experiencing or avoiding (unimportant, guilty, devalued, powerless, inadequate, or unlovable)?
- Are you being as humane and compassionate as you want to be? Do you think the other people involved in this situation are more frail than cruel or evil?
- Describe what you will due to improve the situation you described. Can you improve this situation? If you can't improve the situation, describe what you can due to improve your experience of it (i.e., how can you make it more pleasant or less uncomfortable for yourself?).

Not all of these questions should be addressed in every journal entry, but rather, these should be considered as students deal with tough or highly emotional events or situations. Having the student address some of these questions can turn a negative journal entry into a more positive learning experience for the child.

Handling Dangerous Events Described in Journal Entries

Another issue in usiurnals involves dealing with illegal events or dangerous content that may come to light in journal entries. It should be obvious that children challenged by trauma often come from homes where something has gone terribly wrong, and one should expect any journal entries from these kids to reflect that reality. Sometimes, those journal entries will bring up matters such as child abuse, violence in the home, parental addictions or other dangerous home conditions, or even dangerous thoughts such as harming oneself or suicidal ideation. Journal entries from kids exposed to trauma are more likely to raise such matters than journal entries from other students. Thus, teachers should consider what happens when dangerous emotions or reflections or even illegal events are described in children's journal entries. Imagine a scenario involving the following journal entry of a sixth-grade boy.

> Last night Mom and her boyfriend were fighting, so I went to my room to play on the Xbox. When I heard a loud bang, I looked out my bedroom door, and Mom was on the floor. Her nose was bleeding when she got up, and then I heard the front door slam. I didn't see the guy anymore, and Mom didn't see me. I was afraid, so I went back into my room, but I cried later that night.

With increased societal awareness of child abuse and neglect, teachers know that any suspicion of violence in the home or child abuse or neglect must be reported to school authorities, and school administration officials may then take appropriate action. As mentioned previously, most school districts have specific reporting forms for teachers or school administration officials to complete, and immediate reporting of these issues is demanded by law.

In the previous scenario, the child clearly experienced some trauma, but it is unclear on other issues. His journal entry does not show that he was directly involved in any physical altercation, but one might correctly point out that being exposed to such potential violence is, in and of itself, traumatic. Clearly witnessing violence is certainly on the "Top 10 List of ACEs," as noted in Chapter 1. Still, the question remains: If teachers see this type of entry in a journal, what do they do?

Of course, children exposed to trauma must be protected whenever any question arises. The safety and growth of the child must be the teacher's and clinician's overriding concern, so for teachers who read a journal entry such as the preceding one, we suggest an immediate discussion with the counselor and school principal. At that point, the principal or counselor might either involve social services or the police or explore the situation further with the student.

For example, should the principal or counselor choose to explore the journal entry further, they might discuss it with the child. Asking open-ended questions like the following can clarify the situation: "What do you mean when you say 'fighting'?" "What did you see and hear?" "What made your mom's nose bleed?" These questions can help educators understand what happened from the child's perspective, and then decisions can be made about potential involvement of youth services and/or the police.

From a counseling perspective, questions that tease out the child's feelings are also useful: "How did you feel that night?" or "What were you thinking about when you started crying?" Sometimes questions about feelings can help professionals understand if the child's fears are rational and are related to specific, actual events. In fact, the child in this situation did not directly witness any violence; that young boy only heard an argument, saw his mother on the floor, and then heard a door slam. Mom might have tripped on something and injured her own face. Further, this child may have cried because he watched a scary movie in the bedroom, and thus the crying may not be related to the adult argument at all. The journal entry merely stated that the child cried later, not that the crying was related to his mom's altercation. In some cases, a few judicious open-ended questions can help clarify a journal entry such as this, thus helping the principal and counselor make appropriate follow-up decisions.

We also suggest that the teacher or clinician write down the time, the date, and the child's answers to whatever questions are asked, as well as preserve the journal entry. That information might become the basis for further inquiry by the appropriate authorities, if the child does, in fact, seem to be in danger.

In the case of a journal entry where there is some ambiguity, as in this student's case, these questions should help provide the professionals with some direction, and again, the safety and growth of the child must be the overriding concern. When a child is not safe, and that is revealed in a journal entry, then the professionals must raise questions, using the journal entry and any notes on questions that were asked, as well as the child's answers, as the evidence for later inquiry and appropriate actions. School district policies typically stipulate what those actions might entail.

Notice we chose to emphasize counselors and principals as the appropriate questioners in this type of situation, while realizing that in some cases experienced teachers may choose to undertake the initial questioning. For early-career teachers, if they feel some questions are warranted but are uneasy asking anything of the child based on their relative inexperience, they might merely take the journal entry to the school counselor or administrator and have that person ask questions of the child and then determine a course of action. Again, the child's safety must be the determining factor in all such decisions.

RESEARCH ON JOURNALING

As noted, research shows that journaling holds many benefits for students of all ages (Greenwald, 2020; Krentzman et al., 2022; Lewis, 2017; Murray, 2002; Sohal, Singh, Dhillon, & Gill, 2022; Ullrich & Lutgendorf, 2002; WebMD, 2021). Further, these benefits center on many of the important issues among kids exposed to trauma, such as the need for trust, the need for control, and the need to reduce stress, as well as improving understanding of moods and emotions. Research has also documented improvements in writing and communication skills, and even shown medical benefits such as strengthening the immune system and healing wounds faster (Dunlap, 2006; Fritson, 2008; Lewis, 2017; O'Connel & Dyment, 2006; Scott, 2023; Ullrich & Lutgendorf, 2002). Further, school journaling has been shown to combat both anxiety and clinical depression while increasing positive moods, increasing social engagement, and improving the quality of close relationships (Grothaus, 2015; Murray, 2002). Each of these researched benefits is a critical concern among students exposed to trauma. Other evidence shows that journaling will help trauma victims experience a sense of greater well-being overall (Tartakovsky, 2022; WebMD, 2021).

Thus, this strategy has very real physical and mental health benefits for challenged kids as well as for all other kids in the class. For children who are victims of trauma, journaling can help them understand that they are in control of their emotions, and thus they are likely to develop an increased sense of personal power. For some victims of trauma, this might come as a singular revelation. Of course, the specific benefits of journaling are dependent on the seriousness of the student during the writing process; the more serious a student is about journaling, the more positive impact the journaling intervention will have.

While research is limited on the clinical use of journaling specifically for students exposed to multiple ACEs, the existing research is positive and has shown that expressive journal writing can even help those recovering from the emotional trauma associated with post-traumatic stress disorder (PTSD) as well as lower their stress overall (Mims, 2015; Sohal et al., 2022; WebMD, 2021). As shown in the extensive research analysis by Sohal et al. (2022), research on both expressive journaling and gratitude journaling as interventions for PTSD, anxiety, and depression show positive, though moderate, effects in 68% of the studies. Finally, according to Sohal and her colleagues (2022), interventions that involved as few as four to six individual journaling sessions resulted in measurable positive impacts for students exposed to trauma.

SUMMARY

Journaling will help children exposed to trauma in many ways, such as reducing stress, alleviating anxieties, and providing an outlet for feelings of frustration and anger. Further, journaling tends to improve both behavior and academic performance at school and can help these children develop a plan for negative events or situations in their lives. Finally, journaling is one of the most effective ways to encourage communication between kids exposed to trauma and teachers, and it can be instrumental in helping the teacher reach these kids in a meaningful way. Journaling, perhaps better than any other strategy, gives students who have experienced trauma a voice—an ability to become an active agent to control their own lives—and that fact alone can be a freeing experience for these students.

For all these reasons, we suggest that virtually all teachers in elementary grades and many teachers in departmentalized schools should implement some type of journaling as a regular, recurring assignment in their class. Teachers and clinicians in an elementary school setting can simply have students in the class write in their journals daily, whereas teachers in departmentalized programs may require at least a weekly journal entry focused on their subject-area topics. Given the stresses that all children face in a post-pandemic world, it is imperative that schools help children cope, and journaling is one tool teachers can use in that regard. In short, the benefits far outweigh the time and other concerns, so almost all elementary and many secondary teachers should be incorporating journaling in their classes.

REFERENCES

Adams, K. (2023). Writing in a journal: A short course on journal writing for 2023. *Center for Journal Therapy*. Retrieved from https://journaltherapy .com/journal-cafe-3/journal-course/

Dunlap, J. C. (2006). Using guided reflective journaling activities to capture students' changing perceptions. *TechTrends, 50*(6), 20–26.

Finley, T. (2010, September 1). The importance of student journals and how to respond efficiently. *Edutopia*. Retrieved from https://www.edutopia.org/ blog/student-journals-efficient-teacher-responses

Fritson, K. K. (2008). Impact of journaling on students' self-efficacy and locus of control. *InSight: A Journal of Scholarly Teaching, 3*, 75–81.

Greenwald, E. (2020, June 19). 8 ways to stop thinking about journaling and actually start journaling. *The Muse*. Retrieved from https://www.themuse .com/advice/8-ways-to-stop-thinking-about-journaling-and-actually-start- journalling

Grothaus, M. (2015, January 29). Why journaling is good for your health (and 8 tips to get better). *Fast Company*. Retrieved from https://www.fastcom pany.com/3041487/8-tips-to-more-effective-journaling-for-health

Krentzman, A. R., Hoeppner, B. B., Hoeppner, S. S., & Barnett, N. P. (2022). Development, feasibility, acceptability, and impact of a positive psychology journaling intervention to support addiction recovery. *The Journal of Positive Psychology, 18*(4), 573–591.

Lewis, B. (2017, June 20). *Journal writing in the elementary classroom*. ThoughtCo. Retrieved from https://www.thoughtco.com/journal-writing-in- the-elementary-classroom-2081069

Mims, R. (2015). Military veteran use of visual journaling during recovery. *Journal of Poetry Therapy*, *29*(2), 99–111.

Murray, B. (2002). Writing to heal. *Monitor on Psychology*, *33*(6), 54–62.

O'Connel, T., & Dyment, J. (2006). Reflections on using journals in higher-education: A focus group discussion with faculty. *Assessment & Evaluation in Higher Education*, *31*(6), 671–691.

Scott, E. (2023, October 26). Why you should keep a stress relief journal. *Verywell Mind*. Retrieved from https://www.verywellmind.com/the-benefits-of-journaling-for-stress-management-3144611

Sohal, M., Singh, P., Dhillon, B. S., & Gill, H. S. (2022). Efficacy of journaling in the management of mental illness: A systematic review and meta-analysis. *Family Medicine and Community Health*, *10*(1), e001154. Retrieved from https://www.doi.org/10.1136/fmch-2021-001154

Stosny, S. (2013, September 6). The good and bad of journaling: Use it as a tool to improve or appreciate. *Psychology Today*. Retrieved from https://www.psychologytoday.com/us/blog/anger-in-the-age-entitlement/201309/the-good-and-the-bad-journaling

Tartakovsky, M. (2022, February 22). 6 journaling benefits and how to start right now. *Healthline*. Retrieved from https://www.healthline.com/health/benefits-of-journaling

Ullrich, P. M., & Lutgendorf, S. K. (2002). Journaling about stressful events: Effects of cognitive processing and emotional expression. *Annals of Behavioral Medicine*, *24*(3), 244–250.

University of Rochester Medical Center. (2024). Journaling for emotional wellness. *Health Encyclopedia*. Retrieved from https://www.urmc.rochester.edu/encyclopedia/content.aspx?ContentID=4552&ContentTypeID=1

WebMD (2021, October 25). *Mental health benefits of journaling*. Retrieved from https://www.webmd.com/mental-health/mental-health-benefits-of-journaling

CHAPTER 8

EMOTIONAL SUPPORT ANIMALS IN THE CLASSROOM

Over the past 10 years, research has increasingly been conducted to assess the effectiveness of animal-assisted intervention (AAI) in the classroom. While this is a more recent strategy for creating a trauma-informed classroom, empirical data indicate it is an effective avenue for increasing confidence, decreasing anxiety, and providing stability for students living in a persistently stressful environment (Kropp & Shupp, 2017). Many components of an AAI program require consideration prior to implementation, but the benefits provide many reasons to work through these concerns. This chapter will focus on the use of therapy dogs in the classroom as part of a comprehensive AAI program. While dogs are not the only choice for AAI in schools, they are the most common choice in school programs and more readily available than other types of programs. Please see Box 8.1 for other options regarding animals that can be used as part of an AAI program if therapy dogs are not accessible for your school.

Box 8.1 Other AAI options

It is important to consider multiple components—the animal's ability to be house-trained, predictability, and ability to engage with humans, for example—when choosing animals to engage in AAI outside of therapy dogs. While smaller animals like cats and ferrets can be supportive of human interaction, their unpredictability disqualifies them from serving as AAI in a school-based environment (Molnár, Iváncsik, DiBlasio, & Nagy, 2019).

Animals to consider include the following:

- Dwarf rabbits are quiet; therefore, they tend not to disturb teaching or classroom environments. Dwarf rabbits can be house-trained and freely move around the classroom (Molnár et al., 2019).

(Continued)

(Continued)

- Guinea pigs are not able to be house-trained, which limits their ability to move about the classroom. While students generally respond positively to the presence of a guinea pig, these animals can be noisy, which can lead to increased disruption in the classroom (Molnár et al., 2019).
- Equine therapy has become increasingly popular as studies have documented its positive effects on child and teen behavior (Pelyva, Kresák, Szóvák, & Tóth, 2020). The opportunity to include equine therapy in most school environments is limited due to cost and space. However, schools should consider having a resource and referral list for students who may benefit from this type of support outside of the school environment.

To implement a therapy dog program, it is important to differentiate between a therapy dog and a service dog. A therapy dog is distinctly different from a service or guide dog. A service dog is a dog trained to provide a specific service for a specific individual in a long-term relationship. Service dogs are trained to support students with medical conditions and may help identify seizures or provide guidance for visually impaired students (Grové, Henderson, Lee, & Wardlaw, 2021). A therapy dog does not provide direct medical support to an individual but instead offers therapeutic benefits through their presence in the working environment (Grové et al., 2021). Therapy dogs are often chosen for the role based on their temperament and then subsequently trained with a handler to be obedient (Grové et al., 2021). Obedience training ensures that the dog is calm and predictable in a variety of environments so that those interacting with the dog can receive emotional support from the dog's presence (Grové et al., 2021). Therapy dogs are a part of a therapeutic environment, working with a professional to achieve a larger goal as part of a tailored program.

BENEFITS OF A THERAPY DOG PROGRAM

Preliminary research indicates that therapy dogs can improve overall well-being in the school setting (Grové et al., 2021). The use of therapy dogs in schools can reduce stress, offer space for connection, and provide a consistent space for acceptance (VonLintel & Bruneau, 2021). Research shows that integrating therapy dogs into the classroom can assist in supporting emotion regulation and can increase opportunities to practice self-control and responsibilities (VonLintel & Bruneau, 2021).

While these benefits are applicable for all students in a classroom, therapy dogs offer unique benefits for students who have experienced trauma. The presence of a predictable animal has been shown to create a sense of safety for those who have experienced trauma (O'Haire, Guérin, & Kirkham, 2015). The presence of the therapy dog signals to these students that they are no longer in danger due to the calm demeanor of the dog in a form of co-regulation (O'Haire et al., 2015). Many students who have been exposed to trauma will experience a consistent and prolonged "freeze" response that reduces emotional expression (O'Haire et al., 2015). The presence of a therapy dog can provoke emotional warmth, reducing the need for isolation and withdrawal (O'Haire et al., 2015).

One of the most common consequences of trauma is a state of consistent hypervigilance as the student's mind is constantly assessing for continued danger. The physical presence of a therapy dog has been shown to promote the release of oxytocin in the brain, which decreases levels of cortisol and produces a calming effect, physically lowering blood pressure (O'Haire et al., 2015). Among the most important benefits of an AAI program are the increased adherence to treatment protocols and the motivation to engage in therapeutic supports in a population that statistically has a higher rate of clients who do not complete therapy recommendations (Muela, Azpiroz, Calzada, Soroa, & Aritzeta, 2019). A study done on clients engaged with therapy dogs showed a 15% increase in behavioral functioning as measured by the Youth Outcomes Questionnaire, which assesses treatment progress and effectiveness (O'Haire et al., 2015).

IMPLEMENTING AN AAI PROGRAM

There are multiple ways to integrate a therapy dog into a school program to create a trauma-informed environment. Before beginning the program, the school must establish the overall goal of the AAI. The goal of program implementation should be clear including detailed understanding of the desired outcomes, who may benefit from the program, and how these benefits will occur (Grové et al., 2021). Once these goals are established, the school administration can identify the appropriate frequency and duration of visits and the activities that the therapy dog will support (Grové et al., 2021). Having a clear understanding of desired outcomes also helps assess the effectiveness of the program and identify any necessary modifications.

One of the most difficult components of introducing AAI in a school is identifying students who will benefit the most from the program. Logistical considerations must include ensuring that all students identified for the program are able to engage with the therapy dog without concern for cultural or religious beliefs, allergies, or fears (Grové et al., 2021). Any student chosen to participate in the program will also need time for education to ensure proper and safe engagement with the therapy dog. Finally, once the intended population is identified, the administration must determine if the program will be structured as a whole-class program, small-group program, or individual support program (Grové et al., 2021).

The school must also identify an effective lead staff member to take on the responsibility of the program (Grové et al., 2021). Implementation of an AAI program will require a time commitment for the program to be successful. The lead staff member will work to ensure program goals are clear, school staff and students are adequately prepared for the therapy dog visit, and appropriate environments for animal–student interaction are identified (Grové et al., 2021). In addition, the lead staff member must be acutely aware of the school population to be sensitive to diversity, perceptions about animals, and allergies (Grové et al., 2021).

Prior to implementing AAI, all stakeholders must be prepared including staff, students, and parents (Grové et al., 2021). The program lead not only must ensure that all stakeholders have had adequate time to understand the goals of the program and provide feedback, but must be made aware of any aversion to AAI including traumatic experiences of staff or students as well as allergies, cultural conflicts, or religious concerns. These must be considered with specific guidelines on how these concerns will be respected. For example, if a student or staff member has had a traumatic experience relating to a dog, the therapy dog may need to be on a leash at all times when outside of the handler's immediate classroom or office. This provides an increased sense of safety and predictability for those with dog aversion. Students and staff may need to know the dog will not be in their immediate environment for increased comfort in the school building. Students in need of AAI support who are in a classroom with dog-averse stakeholders will require movement to a different location to engage with the therapy dog. One of the easiest ways to begin using a therapy dog approach in the school is to research volunteer organizations that provide certified handlers and trained therapy dogs (VonLintel & Bruneau, 2021). Handlers and their dogs have been trained and evaluated through the volunteer program and have demonstrated an ability to effectively work together in a variety of environments. Dogs are trained and assessed to consistently obey the handler and can be trusted for predictability in a classroom setting. This is a cost-effective starting point for the school to assess the overall fit and effectiveness of an AAI program prior to working toward always having a handler and therapy dog on school grounds. Box 8.2 presents several organizations that might be consulted.

Box 8.2 Volunteer organizations for AAI

These organizations are sponsored by the American Kennel Club:

- Alliance of Therapy Dogs
- Pet Partners
- Love on a Leash
- Bright and Beautiful Therapy Dogs
- Therapy Dogs International

Schools may also work toward having a full-time staff member become a certified handler. The handler and the therapy dog must receive adequate training and evaluation prior to implementation in the school program. The dog must be agreeable to people, predictable in a variety of settings, and adaptable (Grové et al., 2021). The handler must prepare to be responsible for the dog's welfare at all times, including ensuring the dog is safe, has adequate breaks, meets hygiene requirements, and is up to date on all vaccinations (Grové et al., 2021).

PROGRAMMING OPTIONS

While there are multiple ways to incorporate AAI in a school setting, the purposes of program planning for this literature is focused on social-emotional interventions for supplementing a trauma-informed environment. In most settings, working alongside the school counselor for implementation of these programs ensures that the social-emotional goals are being met. In outlining AAI for a trauma-informed classroom, we present several ways that therapy dogs can specifically support students who have experienced trauma.

School Refusal

School refusal is defined as a repetitive refusal to attend school or remain in the school building for the required amount of time per day. While school refusal is not a diagnosis outlined in the *Diagnostic and Statistical Manual of Mental*

Disorders (DSM-5-TR; American Psychiatric Association, 2022), it can be a symptom that manifests as a part of other diagnoses including separation anxiety, social anxiety, acute stress disorder, post-traumatic stress disorder, specific phobia, or major depressive disorder (Kawsar, Yilanli, & Marwaha, 2022). School refusal has many negative consequences for the student including a significant impact on the student's social, emotional, and academic growth (Kawsar et al., 2022).

While a student who has experienced trauma may show symptoms of school refusal for a myriad of reasons, one may be an effort to control their environment for increased predictability and stability. The need for control among students exposed to trauma has been discussed previously, but one way to address that need is through AAI. To increase consistency in school attendance, counselors can incorporate predictable visits with the therapy dog as part of the student's schedule. These predictable visits provide the student with an incentive for classroom and school attendance. School counselors can work with the classroom teacher and the student to identify a predictable schedule that includes visual prompts indicating time with the therapy dog. This schedule will be provided to the student for an at-home and in-class visual so that the student is aware of each day's structure. During these visits, the student can have time with the dog that is individualized for the student's needs. Visits may include walks around the school grounds, time for petting in an isolated area, or time to read to the dog. Providing the student autonomy in the way these visits are structured aligns with guidelines for trauma-informed care outlined by the Centers for Disease Control and Prevention (Office of Readiness and Response, 2020).

Increased Hyperarousal

One significant symptom of trauma exposure is hyperarousal, a chronically heighted state of the autonomic nervous system preparing a student for "fight, flight, or freeze." Physiological symptoms of hyperarousal may include accelerated heart rates, increased blood pressure, and shortness of breath. Students experiencing prolonged periods of hyperarousal may be irritable and have difficulty attaining the appropriate amount of sleep each night, resulting in decreased ability to concentrate in school (Danese, McLaughlin, Samara, & Stover, 2020). Studies show that physical contact between a human and an animal can increase levels of oxytocin in the body (Beetz, Schöfmann, Girgensohn, Braas, & Ernst, 2019). An increase in oxytocin in the body has been shown to reduce stress parameters, including a reduction in blood pressure, heart rate, and cortisol levels (Beetz et al., 2019). Levels of oxytocin released are shown to be higher if the student and the animal have an ongoing relationship (Beetz et al., 2019).

For students experiencing continued hyperarousal due to trauma exposure, the inclusion of a therapy dog as part of a trauma-informed school provides a safe space for helping them achieve a calm state. The use of a therapy dog in this situation will be aligned with the school's work on emotion identification and effective coping skills. Students will work with the counselor or support personnel to appropriately and accurately identify how their body feels when it is entering a hypervigilant state. Students will then identify how to seek support prior to dysregulation aligned with their body cues. With AAI, the student will identify a plan to seek individual time with the school's therapy dog to help regulate the autonomic nervous system. Given that this occurs on an as-needed basis, this type of AAI will be more aligned with a school that has access to a full-time therapy dog. The plan for the student needs to be outlined specifically with details on how to request time with the therapy animal, and should identify other effective coping skills to implement if the therapy dog is unavailable. Given that the impact of the therapy dog is greater if there is an ongoing relationship, this type of AAI will be most helpful if combined with regular visits for the student to increase the child's connection with the dog prior to use in a dysregulated state.

Isolation

Studies have indicated that exposure to trauma in childhood and adolescence is a predictive factor for increased experiences of loneliness throughout the life span (Landry, Asokumar, Crump, Anisman, & Matheson, 2022). In particular, research has shown that abuse in early childhood is aligned with increased experiences of loneliness in young adult life (Landry et al., 2022). For students who have experienced trauma, feelings of social indifference may lead to increased isolation in the school environment (Landry et al., 2022). For these students, this may look like decreased engagement in structured group settings or less interaction with peers in unstructured settings such as the playground or cafeteria. Students who have experienced trauma in the form of emotional abuse from caregivers may experience lower self-esteem due to self-blame (Landry et al., 2022). These students will have a more difficult time engaging in social activities that would provide for friendships, social support, and community. Students who have experienced physical and emotional abuse may develop avoidant, anxious, or disorganized attachment styles, making it difficult to maintain friendships with peers or mentors.

For students experiencing any form of isolation, research shows that AAI can assist in creating secure connections (Dell & Poole, 2015). Physical contact is a basic human need that can be met for a student with a therapy dog without fear of trauma reminders or increased hyperarousal (Dell & Poole, 2015). For these students, counselors can incorporate independent time with the therapy dog for opportunities to build trust in engagement. Students who avoid physical contact will need a setting that is stable and predictable without distractions or sudden interruptions. It will be important to provide the student with autonomy to lead the interactions. Depending on the student's level of engagement, it may be necessary to start with activities that do not require close physical contact such as reading to the dog or taking the dog for a walk. The student can then slowly be introduced to more intimate activities such as petting the dog or allowing the dog to sit on the same couch while reading aloud. From there, the student could engage in increased contact such as brushing or feeding the therapy dog.

For students who routinely disengage with peers in nonstructured settings, AAI can increase opportunities for social connection. Studies of AAI indicate that therapy dogs can be used as a catalyst for social connection (Grové et al., 2021). Therapy dogs can promote prosocial behaviors as students have the opportunity to engage in conversation around a specific topic that is familiar and links students despite backgrounds. Counselors can initiate various programs to encourage social connection using the therapy dog as a common factor. Incorporating the therapy dog into weekly social groups provides a consistent space for students to join with others building connection. The students may use the dog to practice mindfulness activities (e.g., sit near the dog and notice what you see, feel, hear, or smell). Students may use the dog as a catalyst for emotion identification (e.g., how do you feel when you see the dog in the hallways? How do you feel when you pet the dog?). During these activities, students can normalize their reactions, and the counselor can link their responses to increase feelings of connection with other students in the school (Grové et al., 2021).

SUMMARY

The use of AAI has shown numerous benefits for entire school communities in a variety of ways from increased academic engagement to trauma support (Grové et al., 2021). While various steps must be taken prior to implementation, the multifaceted uses available for AAI outweigh the initial work required to start an effective program. Schools will need adequate time to identify a lead administrator for the program, identify an appropriate therapy dog, incorporate and inform stakeholders, and create the appropriate environment for the therapy dog. Schools can utilize volunteer organizations that are familiar with AAI to help with program implementation. While this chapter has outlined basic program guidelines, schools considering the use of AAI may want to consider purchasing and using the *Handbook on Animal-Assisted Therapy* edited by Aubrey H. Fine (2019) as a guidebook for specific considerations. This book provides conceptual guidelines for quality programming and can be used as a resource for stakeholders.

REFERENCES

American Psychiatric Association. (2022). *Diagnostic and statistical manual of mental disorders.* (5th ed. text rev.). American Psychiatric Association.

Beetz, A., Schöfmann, I., Girgensohn, R., Braas, R., & Ernst, C. (2019). Positive effects of a short-term dog-assisted intervention for soldiers with post-traumatic stress disorder—A pilot study. *Frontiers in Veterinary Science, 6.* doi:10.3389/fvets.2019.00170

Danese, A., McLaughlin, K. A., Samara, M., & Stover, C. S. (2020). Psychopathology in children exposed to trauma: Detection and intervention needed to reduce downstream burden. *The BMJ, 2020*(371), m3073. doi: 10.1136/bmj.m3073

Dell, C. A., & Poole, N. (2015). Taking a PAWS to reflect on how the work of a therapy dog supports a Trauma-Informed approach to prisoner health. *Journal of Forensic Nursing, 11*(3), 167–173. doi:10.1097/jfn.0000000000 000074

Fine, A. H. (2019). *Handbook on animal-assisted therapy: Foundations and guidelines for animal-assisted interventions.* Academic Press.

Grové, C., Henderson, L., Lee, F., & Wardlaw, P. (2021). Therapy dogs in educational settings: Guidelines and recommendations for implementation. *Frontiers in Veterinary Science, 8.* doi:10.3389/fvets.2021.655104

Kawsar, M. S., Yilanli, M., & Marwaha, R. (2022, June 5). *School refusal.* StatPearls: National Center for Biotechnology Information Bookshelf. Retrieved from https://www.ncbi.nlm.nih.gov/books/NBK534195/

Kropp, J., & Shupp, M. (2017). Review of the research: Are therapy dogs in classrooms beneficial? *Forum on Public Policy Online, 2017*(2), EJ1173578. Retrieved from https://files.eric.ed.gov/fulltext/EJ1173578.pdf

Landry, J., Asokumar, A., Crump, C., Anisman, H., & Matheson, K. (2022). Early life adverse experiences and loneliness among young adults: The mediating role of social processes. *Frontiers in Psychology, 13*, 968383. doi:10.3389/ fpsyg.2022.968383

Molnár, M., Iváncsik, R., DiBlasio, B., & Nagy, I. (2019). Examining the effects of rabbit-assisted interventions in the classroom environment. *Animals*, *10*(1), 26. doi:10.3390/ani10010026

Muela, A., Azpiroz, J., Calzada, N., Soroa, G., & Aritzeta, A. (2019). Leaving a mark, an animal-assisted intervention programme for children who have been exposed to gender-based violence: A pilot study. *International Journal of Environmental Research and Public Health*, *16*(21), 4084. doi:10.3390/ijerph16214084

Office of Readiness and Response. (2020, September 17). *Infographic: 6 guiding principles to a trauma-informed approach*. U.S. Department of Health and Human Services, Centers for Disease Control and Prevention. Retrieved from https://www.cdc.gov/orr/infographics/6_principles_trauma_info.htm

O'Haire, M. E., Guérin, N. A., & Kirkham, A. C. (2015). Animal-assisted intervention for trauma: A systematic literature review. *Frontiers in Psychology*, *6*. doi:10.3389/fpsyg.2015.01121

Pelyva, I. Z., Kresák, R., Szovák, E., & Tóth, A. (2020). How equine-assisted activities affect the prosocial behavior of adolescents. *International Journal of Environmental Research and Public Health*, *17*(8), 2967. doi:10.3390/ijerph17082967

VonLintel, J., & Bruneau, L. (2021). Pathways for implementing a school therapy dog program: Steps for success and best practice considerations. *Journal of School Counseling*, *19*(14), EJ1301291. Retrieved from https://files.eric.ed.gov/fulltext/EJ1301291.pdf

CHAPTER 9

MENTORING STUDENTS EXPOSED TO TRAUMA

MENTORING IN SCHOOLS

The Need for Mentors

As one might suspect, many students exposed to trauma lack effective and appropriate adult role models in their homes. Parents or relatives who are in the home, in many cases, do not display the types of personal skills, interpersonal skills, discipline skills, or caring behaviors that nurture children appropriately. Thus, providing effective role models for kids exposed to trauma can be one of the most important interventions undertaken at the school level, and recently, schoolwide mentoring programs have been emphasized as one way to provide such role models to children exposed to trauma (Gordon, Downey, & Bangert, 2013; Jucovy, Garringer, & MacRae, 2008; Sox & Min, 2023; Youth Collaboratory, 2019).

Mentoring programs in general were emphasized under the administration of President Bill Clinton in the late 1990s as the nation was seeking appropriate responses to increased school violence and random shootings in schools (Bender, 2007). Since that time, mentoring programs in schools have been used with some success in curbing serious behavior problems and as dropout prevention programs (Adams, 2014; Lawner, Beltz, & Moore, 2013; Vanderwerf, 2014). Whereas some mentoring programs involve older school students mentoring younger students, others involve the use of adult mentors, and both types of mentoring programs seem to work (Lawner et al., 2013). However, children exposed to trauma present many more challenges for a mentor than do other kids, and these children are likely to respond better when the mentor is more mature (Sox & Min, 2023).

Adult mentoring involves using adults from the local community to partner with students experiencing behavioral difficulties in the school setting. This concept has been described as a one-to-one relationship between an adult and a younger person who are not relatives and whose relationship is formed to support the younger person during their youth (Sox & Min, 2023; Youth Collaboratory, 2019). Of course, there are many ways in which children can be traumatized, but regardless of the type of childhood trauma to which children might be exposed, research has shown that a caring adult who bonds with a student and is available to the student over time can become a significant resilience factor and positively influence the direction of that student's behavior and overall social development (Lawner et al., 2013; Lippman & Schmitz, 2013; Sox & Min, 2023; Vanderwerf, 2014).

In addition to offering support for kids in crisis, adult mentors can often provide a basis for sustained self-reflection on behavior and even internal rage, and often this strategy will work with violent or aggressive children exposed to trauma even when other strategies fail (Sox & Min, 2023; Vanderwerf, 2014). Further, the body of research on resilience among children exposed to trauma shows that a caring, involved adult can be the single most important factor in promoting more normal social adjustment for these children (Adams, 2014; Lippman & Schmitz, 2013). Clearly, in serving students exposed to trauma, an adult mentoring program is something that should be considered essential within the trauma-informed school.

A Mentoring Miracle

Dr. Bender was privileged a few years ago to see a highly effective adult mentoring program in action. He was hosting a Georgia Public Broadcasting show on educational innovations, and he had the opportunity to interview several participating mentors and children in the mentoring program in Greene County, Georgia. The elementary and middle school faculty there had seen an increasing trend toward rage and classroom violence and, as a response, had undertaken a mentoring program by inviting citizens in the community to "come into our school and change a kid's life!" Many of those persons were retired teachers (Clinton & Miles, 1999).

Vignette 9.1 A mentoring miracle

Mr. Willie Miles, principal of Greene County Elementary School, had spoken to a number of civic clubs and churches to find mentors, telling those citizens that there was a great need for effective role models for many troubled kids in their schools and that they could make a positive difference in a single kid's life—and ultimately in the

Vignette 9.1 (Continued)

local community. At the first mentoring training meeting two months later, Mr. Miles was expecting 21 people in attendance: adults who had agreed to show up for the training and begin to mentor a child. However, they were overwhelmed that first evening when over 80 adults stepped into that room to receive the training! Mr. Miles was overjoyed (he immediately ordered more snacks to feed them all!). The next morning, with so many potential mentors at hand, he said that he had to search his disciplinary referral records to find 60 additional names of kids who could benefit from mentoring. He felt that the need to find more kids was a wonderful problem to have. Those volunteers, men and women, many retired teachers, had each stepped up to the call to give back to their community by helping one student in need. Mr. Miles considered that mentor training evening, and the subsequent mentoring program, to be nothing less than a miracle.

(Bender, 2007; Clinton & Miles, 1999)

Within a year, that entire school faculty supported the adult mentoring program. In fact, at Mr. Miles's suggestion, each teacher agreed to take one or two additional kids into their class, in order to "spring" a veteran teacher from class responsibilities for the entire morning so that they might manage that mentoring program. Those teachers clearly believed that adult mentoring drastically improved behavior in their classes and the overall school climate. Thus, they were willing to take the extra kids each year (Clinton & Miles, 1999). We have every confidence that this strategy can and will do the same in your school.

FACTORS TO CONSIDER IN MENTORING

Same-Sex/Same-Race Mentoring

Mentoring primarily involves providing an appropriate adult role model to a student with behavioral problems, including students exposed to trauma, in order for a positive relationship to develop between the mentor and the student. There are many advantages to such a relationship. However, to increase the likelihood of creating a strong relationship, schools should consider various factors. First, psychologists have traditionally emphasized the critical influence of same-sex, same-race role models to assist children in becoming successful adults (Bender, 2007). Students seem to bond better with a role model who is "like" them. Therefore, if possible, schools should plan their mentoring efforts around pairing troubled students with mentors of the same sex and race. However, it is often the case that schools find more female than male mentors, so partnering students with mentors of the opposite sex may be necessary. Likewise, same-race mentors may be difficult to find, and mentoring should nevertheless proceed for as many students as possible.

Mentoring Outside of School

While most mentoring efforts are based around the mentor "tutoring" the student during class time (Vanderwerf, 2014), the most important aspect of mentorship is not instruction, but rather building a positive rapport with a student exposed to trauma (Bender, 2007). The most effective mentorships move far beyond this "tutoring only" dynamic to explore the areas of mutual interest or hobbies. Again, it is not academic content around which a mentorship is structured, but the intensity of the relationship between the mentor and the student that is more important for kids exposed to trauma.

Given the importance of the intensity of the relationship, schools must consider what mentoring consists of. For example, most mentoring programs involve adults mentoring students in school, during school hours, but some mentors may wish to build more involved relationships with their students. Perhaps a mentor wants to take a student to a local football game on Friday evening, or maybe on a church camping trip. This was frequently the case in the Greene County example described previously. Of course, this also raises the question, what are mentors allowed to do with their mentees? Further, this outside activity issue brings up certain liability concerns for the school.

First, more involved, appropriate relationships can greatly benefit the students as long as mentors do not overstep any obvious boundaries. Thus, the Friday night football game type of outing should be encouraged, with certain provisions. Schools should certainly complete a police background check of each mentor, prior to assigning mentors and students together. Also, mentors must be required to always obtain permission directly from parents for such activities.

Finally, to address the liability issue in the case of Greene County, all parents of mentees were required to sign a permission form prior to their children participating in mentoring. On that form, they were specifically told that "all mentor activities will take place during school hours and on school property." The form also stated that, "if the parents choose to allow their child to participate in after-school activities with the mentor, those activities are entirely at the parents' discretion and are not to be considered part of the mentoring program." Thus, the school board attorney believed that the form provided legal protection, relative to various liability concerns.

School Personnel as Mentors

Some schools implement adult mentoring on the basis of partnering troubled students with school personnel. Vanderwerf (2014) described a successful program in which teachers, school administrators, and others on campus are partnered with challenged youth. This strategy can work well because those on-campus educators already know the kids and have extensive experience with them. However, the major difficulty here is obvious: There may not be enough mentors and/or enough mentoring time. Schools are welcome to use their faculty as mentors if they wish, but in almost all mentoring programs, the time and availability of mentors is often a concern. Thus, using adult mentors from the community should be considered as one supplemental option.

Duration of the Mentorship

The duration of the mentoring experience is another factor to consider. Although mentoring can be effective during half-year mentoring programs, mentoring is more likely to be effective if it lasts a year or longer (Lawner et al., 2013). Specifically, Lawner and her colleagues (2013) showed that adult mentoring programs based on weekly meetings over a full year were more likely to be effective than shorter programs. Further, other research shows that the rapport between mentors and mentees grew stronger among programs that allowed the mentor relationship to continue for more than one year (Gordon et al., 2013). Clearly, if trust is established within a mentor and mentee pair in one year, there are many advantages to continuing that same relationship during the next year. Also, Sox and Min (2023) indicated that when mentoring is used with students exposed to trauma, mentoring that lasts longer than a year is preferable, as these students will be slower to open up with their mentors than other students.

In the Greene County example, some mentors chose to remain with their selected students for two or even three years. Further, in that example, the mentoring program itself actually "graduated." After several years mentoring, the school principal, Mr. Miles, got a call from an administrator at the local junior high school. That principal, pretending to be somewhat agitated, opened the conversation, saying, "Willie, we don't have a mentoring program here, but because of you, I have to start one!" Mr. Miles responded that his mentoring program was working wonderfully, and that his faculty loved the program, but that he was certainly not attempting to force that idea on any other school in the district. The other principal replied, "No, you're not, but your mentors sure are!"

Apparently, a couple of mentors who had been working with "their" students for several years in Mr. Miles's school found that their students were moving on to junior high. That next fall, they simply showed up at the junior high school and asked when they could plan to mentor their students! When told that the junior high did not have a mentoring program, one of those mentors merely smiled and said, "You do now!" This speaks to the development of a very positive relationship between mentor and mentee, and the unanticipated "graduation" of a mentoring program would be a wonderful problem to have in any school district. On a more serious note, for students exposed to trauma, this strong, warm relationship with an adult mentor is exactly what they need.

Mentor Training

Another factor to consider is the training of mentors. Retired teachers, of course, are accustomed to working with students and understand the various challenges that may arise, but other adults may not be, so some training will be in order. Research shows that programs that provide training and support for mentors work better than programs that offer no training (Lawner et al., 2013), and generally two or three hours of training on at least two evenings prior to beginning mentoring is recommended as a minimum. That time frame will allow schools to undertake a police background check on the prospective mentors and to review school policy on what a mentor should and should not do when a mentee becomes noncompliant. Some schools offer mentor training on an ongoing basis, and this allows those schools to initiate new mentors throughout the school year. Much of this can be done via online sources, and a number of these resources are described on the companion website for this book (https://traumahelpnow.com).

Of course, no mentor should ever consider using corporal punishment even when such practices are allowed by district policy. We would also suggest that no mentor should ever institute any punishment at all when mentoring a child. However, knowing how the mentor should report problems that may arise during the mentor session will be of benefit, and must be covered in pre-mentor training. It is also a good idea, during the second or third mentor training session, for the perspective mentees and parents to be invited to meet the mentors.

For mentors working with children exposed to trauma, additional training on trauma-informed school practices is essential (Sox & Min, 2023). Those mentors should be explicitly taught to view their child's behavior through the lens of the child's exposure to trauma (Sox & Min, 2023; Youth Collaboratory, 2019), and they must understand that any small "success" is a huge success with these kids.

Further, this training should emphasize avoidance of "re-traumatization" of the student. Re-traumatization is defined as reaction to a current event based on exposure to previous trauma and similarities between the original trauma and the current situation. Of course, trauma-informed mentors must be trained to avoid known triggers for various traumas, as well as to exercise extreme caution should a student wish to open up about their trauma (Youth Collaboratory, 2019). Mentors should avoid, for example, asking questions about previous trauma or a student's home environment, which may trigger re-traumatization. In short, trauma-informed practices are as important, if not more so, for mentors than for teachers, and this will require appropriate training.

ADMINISTRATION AND PROGRAM STRUCTURE

The Mentor Coordinator

Depending on the number of adult mentors entering the school, a mentor coordinator may be assigned for half a day or perhaps a full day to administer the mentoring program. That trained school professional should remain in the classroom or library where mentors are working with their mentees and, thus, be able to intervene should a behavior problem arise during that mentoring. Further, mentors will need a contact phone number or email for situations in which they need to miss a day. Without good leadership and coordination, any adult mentoring program is likely to fail, and as more mentors work with more kids, the administrative demands only increase. The tasks of the mentoring coordinator are many and varied, but some of those tasks are found in Box 9.1.

Box 9.1 Role of mentor coordinator

- Develop goals and objectives for the program
- Recruit mentors
- Identify (with the principal) students for mentoring
- Match mentors to students

(Continued)

(Continued)

- Write guidelines for mentors
- Provide support for mentors
- Collect data for objectives on the mentoring plan
- Schedule mentoring activities
- Report results each semester on the program

IDENTIFICATION OF GOALS AND OBJECTIVES

Program efficacy will be measured based on specific goals and objectives of the program, and in the initial planning stages, educators should develop a list of desired goals. These goals and objectives may range from reducing behavioral problem referrals, to improving mental health, to reducing dropouts. Other issues may suggest program goals, such as a higher-than-average teenage pregnancy rate, high levels of overt aggression, or a need for more respect for others. The concerns of the faculty provide a good place to begin when establishing program goals, and those goals, once identified, will ultimately help focus the mentoring program. Box 9.2 presents some examples of program goals and specific objectives for a mentoring program at a middle school.

Box 9.2 Examples of goals and objectives of a mentoring program

Examples of Program Goals

- To decrease office referrals for behavior problems by 30%
- To decrease in-school (or out-of-school) suspensions by 50%
- To decrease the likelihood of aggressive behavior by a student by 50%
- To increase student attendance by 20%
- To increase academic achievement by 10%

Examples of Specific Objectives

- By the fourth week of the mentor recruitment/training period, 30 volunteer mentors will have been screened and enrolled in the program.
- By the October 1 launch date, all mentor/student pairs will be assigned.

- By the seventh week after October 1, 9 out of 10 students will have attended 80% of their meetings with mentors.
- By the ninth week after October 1, 8 out 10 students will have mastered the first vocational skill area assigned (e.g., job application forms).
- By the ninth week after October 1, each mentor will have at least one conversation with their student about choosing alternatives to inappropriate behaviors at school.
- By the end of the first year, the majority of the mentored students will have increased their reading proficiency by at least one grade level.
- By the end of the first year, incidents of aggressive or violent behavior resulting in office disciplinary referrals involving students in the program will have decreased by 50%.

Which Students Participate?

The number of mentors in many programs is quite limited, and this often dictates the number of students who can be served. However, there is still the question of which students should receive mentoring. Does a particular elementary or secondary grade need intensive help? For example, some high schools might prioritize the incoming ninth-grade class for their mentoring efforts rather than eleventh graders or seniors. Another question is whether special education populations (e.g., kids with learning or physical disabilities, pregnant teens) should participate in mentoring. In particular, students identified with special needs are already receiving individualized attention, and many schools do not include such students in the mentoring program for that reason.

When it comes to students exposed to trauma, some of those students may be in special education programs whereas others may not be. Also, Sox and Min (2023) report that they found a shorter duration of mentoring among students exposed to trauma, because many mentors felt that they were just not capable of working with students with such intensive needs. With that concern noted, the need for trauma-informed mentorship training becomes even more obvious. Mentor coordinators should typically pair their strongest, most experienced mentors with students exposed to multiple adverse childhood experiences (ACEs). For these reasons, administrators and mentor coordinators will have to make decisions on student participants on an individual basis.

Resources for Mentoring

Mentors at the school will need to know where to take their mentee during a school mentoring session. Optimally, a classroom might be made available for this program, or at least a workspace in the media center, the cafeteria, or elsewhere. Typically, initial tutoring of mentees will utilize the books and materials provided in other classes, so there are usually no materials costs. Also, if existing mentor programs can be identified in the district, they can provide a resource for the school faculty; they might visit those schools to see how they managed the resource issues for mentoring.

Of course, funding in any amount will help get a new mentorship program off the ground. Educators may consider Title I funds, state grants, parent–teacher associations (PTAs), Kiwanis International, and other community service organizations, local corporations, or corporate foundations. These organizations are also excellent places to seek out appropriate adult mentors. Further, industry in the local area should be consulted since some businesses offer a "release time" for employees to conduct mentoring, or perhaps even some financial support for mentoring programs.

SETTING UP A SCHOOLWIDE MENTORING PROGRAM

A number of sources provide information on mentoring programs (Bender, 2007; Clinton & Miles, 1999; Sox & Min, 2023; Vanderwerf, 2014; Youth Collaboratory, 2019). Of course, specific steps to implement a program vary from one program to another, but most mentoring programs involve the following tasks.

Select an Advisory Board

An advisory board comprising school staff, mentors, parents, and the administrator should be set up to guide the mentoring program. A smaller group is usually most efficient, and many schools function with only the principal and mentor coordinator on this committee. Still, a considerable amount of work is initially involved in recruiting mentors and setting up training, so schools may wish to include others on the advisory board. For example, local ministers and faith leaders, business leaders, PTA representatives, and so on may be of great assistance in guiding the mentoring efforts, not to mention in finding appropriate adult mentors for the school.

Develop General Guidelines for Mentors

The advisory committee and mentor coordinator need to delineate procedures for mentors in some detail. For example, the kind of relationship expected might be described (e.g., at school, or school and community). Box 9.3 presents some examples that help set the parameters for the mentoring experience (Bender, 2007). Any prospective guidelines for the mentoring experience must, of course, be consistent with all school and school board policies.

> ## Box 9.3 Guidelines and expectations of mentors
>
> - Must agree to undergo a police background check and are expected to relate to their mentees in an ethically appropriate, caring, and professional manner.
> - Schedule a specific day and time each week for their mentoring, and make every weekly mentoring appointment.
> - Call the school on each mentoring day to find out if the student is present. If the student is absent, mentors should reschedule their mentoring time when the student returns to school.
> - Sign in at the school office when they arrive at school.
> - Pick up the student from their classroom, checking with the teacher concerning any special events of concern.
> - Proceed with the student to the mentoring center classroom, where the mentoring coordinator supervises the mentoring period.
> - Bring any concern, problem, or observed misbehavior by the student to the attention of the mentoring coordinator.
> - Assist the mentoring coordinator in collecting performance data relative to goals and objectives of the mentoring program.
> - Give small gifts to their students on occasion. If there is a time when mentors would like to give the students a special gift (e.g., holiday, birthday), the mentoring coordinator must approve the timing and the gift, so as not to result in jealousy among the students.
> - Realize that all information such as class test scores, behavior problems, and family structure regarding students is confidential.
> - Attend monthly instructional meetings (e.g., all mentors meet on the second Wednesday at 4:30 p.m. in the mentoring center). The mentors will discuss achievements, concerns, or plans. Also, this is where mentors might pick up ideas from other mentors. Ongoing training sessions for new mentors will take place during regular monthly meetings.

Identify Initial Mentors and Mentoring Activities

Obtaining mentors for 10%–15% of a school population is no small matter, but partnering mentors with children who repeatedly show up in the office on disciplinary referrals will make a positive difference in the number of such referrals. This understanding makes the task of finding mentors much less onerous. Administrators and mentor coordinators should invite adult mentors from local industry, all community faith-based organizations, and all civic clubs (PTA, Lions, Elks, Moose, pilot clubs, garden clubs, etc.). At each event, administrators should try to get individuals to sign up for the mentorship program. That tentative count will provide some information to help plan the first evening of mentor training.

Evidence of Efficacy in Adult Mentoring

In schools today, decisions must be data-driven, and educational innovations must be based on hard data. Educators must be expected to collect data on how mentees' behavior, social skills, and/or grades may change once they begin a mentoring program. The mentor coordinator will aggregate these data and develop periodic reports on the impact of the mentoring program by focusing on the goals and objectives delineated. The reports should include data on improvements in individual student behaviors as well as any specific evidence for program efficacy that teachers provide. Most principals aggregate data on office referrals over a given year, and that information should be compared to the same indicator prior to implementation of the mentoring program.

For some students exposed to trauma, indicators of improved school attendance, improved behavior, and social skills will be one result of the mentoring program. These data showing success should certainly be shared with the student's caregiver as well as the student. Such data will tend to show that students can improve their behavior and have more control over their level of success in school, and for those students, such information is critical.

RESEARCH ON ADULT MENTORING

Overall, the available research evidence shows that adult mentoring works for students with behavioral and mental health problems, including students exposed to trauma (Gordon et al., 2013; Jucovy et al., 2008; Lawner et al., 2013; Sox & Min, 2023; Vanderwerf, 2014). As one example, in 2013, Lawner and her colleagues evaluated the efficacy research for 19 school mentoring programs. Among those, 15 programs focused on educational goals, and 10 of those programs showed a positive impact for at least one educational outcome. For programs focused on decreasing risky behaviors, 7 out of 9 worked. However, of the 11 programs that measured the impact of mentoring on severe behavioral problems (e.g., delinquency, overt aggression), only 2 showed a positive impact in that review (Lawner et al., 2013).

In contrast, other studies demonstrate efficacy of mentoring programs in exactly these problem behavior areas. Gordon and colleagues (2013) examined the efficacy of mentoring among sixth- through ninth-grade students and measured social and behavioral outcomes, including unexcused absences and disciplinary referrals. Positive results were shown on all the outcome variables. In short, while not exclusively positive, the research is supportive of mentoring programs for troubled students, including students exposed to trauma.

SUMMARY

Few schoolwide interventions hold the promise of meeting the needs of kids exposed to trauma, as well as changing the climate of the entire school, as does adult mentoring. For children exposed to trauma, developing a positive relationship with a caring adult can be the most important resilience factor in their lives, and that is why so many schools have undertaken mentoring programs in their efforts to become trauma-informed schools. Still, there is a difference between having 10 or 15 mentors enter a school each week and having 80 such mentors partnered with students exposed to trauma. Clearly, having more well-trained mentors paired with students who are experiencing more challenges will change the school climate much more quickly. If educators wish to change the lives of kids exposed to trauma, as well as initiate a strategy that will fundamentally transform their school climate in a positive manner, this is one of the first strategies they should consider for implementation at a schoolwide level.

REFERENCES

Adams, J. M. (2014, February 3). New "trauma-informed" approach to behavioral disorders in special education. *EdSource*. Retrieved from https://edsource.org/2014/new-trauma-informed-approach-to-behvioral-disorders-in-special-education/56753

Bender, W. N. (2007). *Relational discipline: Strategies for in-your-face kids* (2nd ed.). New Age.

Clinton, G., & Miles, W. (1999). Mentoring programs: Fostering resilience in at-risk kids. In W. Bender, G. Clinton, & R. Bender (Eds.), *Violence prevention and reduction in school* (pp. 31–46). PRO-ED.

Gordon, J., Downey, J., & Bangert, A. (2013). Effects of a school-based mentoring program on school behavior and measures of adolescent connectedness. *School Community Journal, 23*(2), 227–249.

Jucovy, L., Garringer, M., & MacRae, P. (2008). *The ABCs of school based mentoring: Effective strategies for providing quality youth mentoring in school and communities.* The Hamilton Fish Institute on School and Community Violence of the U.S. Department of Justice and The National Mentoring Center at Northwest Regional Educational Laboratory.

Lawner, E., Beltz, M., & Moore, K. A. (2013, March 28). *What works for mentoring programs: Lessons from experimental evaluations of programs and interventions.* Child Trends. Retrieved from https://www.childtrends.org/publications/what-works-for-mentoring-programs-lesson-from-experimental-evaluations-of-programs-and-interventions

Lippman, L., & Schmitz, H. (2013, October 30). *What can schools due to build resilience in their students?* Child Trends. Retrieved from https://www.childtrends.org/what-can-schools-do-to-build-resilience-in-their-students/

Sox, D. M., & Min, H. (2023, January 1). *Mentoring children with traumatic experiences. Youth-Nex.* University of Virginia School of Education and Human Development. Retrieved from https://youthnexblog.education.virginia.edu/?p=2391#

Vanderwerf, L. (2014, January 5). *Willmar Middle School developing mentoring program that aims to keep students in school.* West Central Tribune. Retrieved from https://www.wctrib.com/news/willmar-middle-school-developing-mentoring-program-that-aims-to-keep-students-in-school

Youth Collaboratory. (2019, September 24). *Trauma-informed mentoring.* Wichita State University Center for Combating Human Trafficking. Retrieved from https://www.youthcollaboratory.org/resource/trauma-informed-mentoring

CHAPTER 10

SERVICE LEARNING: HELPING OTHERS TO HELP ONESELF

WHAT IS SERVICE LEARNING?

Service learning is another schoolwide intervention that can be particularly effective with students exposed to trauma. The implementation of various community service programs in public schools began in the 1980s, and later, when schools began to add curricula components to their community service options, true service learning was born (Cheek, 2016; Drew, 2023; Furco, 2011; Knapp & Bradley, 2010; National Center for Education Statistics [NCES], 2023; Spring, Grimm, & Dietz, 2008). The service-learning concept may be defined as students participating in a community service activity in order to master selected course objectives and reflect on the services provided (Drew, 2023; Youth.gov, n.d.). The companion website for this book (https://traumahelpnow.com) includes a list of videos on service learning in schools.

However, the degree of implementation of this approach, the intensity of the learning experience, and the actual duration of the community service were shown to vary greatly among the early programs. Many programs involved weekly hourlong service activities for their students with no curricular requirements. Other schools merely held a "service-learning day" once or twice yearly. Clearly, the distinctions between community service and service learning were quite blurred. Today, service-learning experiences are understood to involve course requirements associated with the community service component and in-depth reflection on the experience (NCES, 2023).

Who Is Doing Service Learning?

Data suggest that 32% of schools in the United States include a service-learning option (NCES, 2023; Spring et al., 2008). According to the NCES (2023), 25% of elementary schools, 38% of middle schools, and 46% of high schools have some students participating in service learning. However, merely having some service learning reported as an option at a school does not mean that all or even most of the students get to participate in those learning opportunities. Some of these programs were required courses while others involved optional participation, and with variations in programs and definitions, student participation numbers are hard to identify. Only Maryland and the District of Columbia included a service-learning requirement for high school graduation (Thomsen, 2014).

Schools in lower-income areas (often defined as schools with over 50% of the children in a free or reduced-price lunch program) are less likely than other schools to have service-learning activities (NCES, 2023; Spring et al., 2008). However, some efficacy data suggest that service learning is very effective with a number of underserved populations, such as children from low-socioeconomic backgrounds and Native American children (Sykes, Pendley, & Deacon, 2017). This would mean that schools should be doing more service learning with these populations, not less.

Types of Service Learning

Historically, service learning has been implemented in a variety of ways. For example, 70% of schools that included service learning reported they used a "grade-wide" model in which all students in one or more grades undertook some service learning (NCES, 2023). However, 62% of schools reported that service learning was offered in individual classes (NCES, 2023). Finally, a "discipline-wide" service-learning model was reported by 53% of the schools (e.g., all history courses or selected English courses in certain grades may include service learning). These figures clearly overlap, as one model is not necessarily exclusive of the other models. With these variations in mind, we would urge educators who are considering implementation of this concept to review some of the videos on service learning listed on the companion website for this book (https://traumahelpnow.com), and then consider how to structure a service-learning curricular component.

SERVICE LEARNING AND STUDENTS EXPOSED TO TRAUMA

This intervention option is most frequently undertaken as a schoolwide intervention because it can be of great benefit to many students, including students exposed to trauma. When educators consider the neurological wiring of kids exposed to trauma, the advantages of some type of service-learning option become apparent. As discussed in Chapter 2, researchers have shown that misbehavior and even overt aggression may be hardwired brain-based responses to perceived threats among children who were repeatedly exposed to trauma, regardless of whether the perceived threat was real (Chemtob, Novaco, Hamada, Gross, & Smith, 1997; Perry, 2000, 2014). Of course, some threats against children in the school environment are real (e.g., bullying, playground violence), but in many cases, the threats perceived by these kids are distorted. The brains of students exposed to trauma all too often function based on perceived threats, and under the distorted perceptions of the lizard brain, survival instinct becomes dominant, leading frequently to aggression and even overt violence (Chemtob et al., 1997; Perry, 2014).

However, the plasticity of the human brain holds the possibility of rewiring such aggressive responses, moving away from aggression or anger as the go-to response and toward a more moderated, reasoned response. This is accomplished through activities that promote peaceful, thorough reflection on events in the environment, which, previously, may have been perceived as threats. In fact, helping others, or any type of altruistic involvement with others, when accomplished in a peaceful manner and coupled with self-reflection on the activity, will help rewire brain responses over time (Doidge, 2007). Even highly aggressive students who explode into violence daily or weekly can be retrained to show different responses, with repeated opportunities to experience a peaceful, safe, helping environment. As children exposed to trauma develop empathy and establish caring, peaceful helping relationships in the service-learning experience, they reprogram the neural connections in their brains in more positive ways. This can be the very thing a child needs to undo some of the neural damage from a childhood characterized by trauma.

SERVICE-LEARNING CONSIDERATIONS

Goals of Service Learning

Different proponents of this strategy have discussed a wide array of goals for service learning (Cheek, 2016; Furco, 2011; Knapp & Bradley, 2010; NCES, 2023; Sykes et al., 2017). These range across the spectrum including the development of interpersonal learning, improved behavior, improved academics, and even increased altruistic behaviors toward other community members (Knapp & Bradley, 2010; National Youth Leadership Council [NYLC], n.d.). Other proponents identify academic goals, such as improved problem solving and deeper reflective thinking, after students have been exposed to long-term service-learning projects. With these goals in mind, service learning clearly holds the potential for helping students, including students exposed to trauma, in a wide variety of ways.

In fact, investigations of service learning have shown explicit transformational outcomes for students in service-learning programs (Conway, Amel, & Gerwien, 2009; Corporation for National and Community Service [CNCS], 2007). Service learning depends on and emphasizes a different manner of learning than more traditional classroom activities, and thus these transformations of self are more likely to result from service-learning activities compared to traditional instruction. In service learning, students are taught to "serve" others in a meaningful, often personal fashion, and in many instances, this will require children exposed to trauma to change their worldview via increased empathy. The 2005 Youth Volunteering and Civic Engagement Survey (CNCS, 2007) demonstrated this exact result. The study found that impoverished students in service-learning programs became more engaged overall, and that their belief in their own ability to make a positive difference in their community grew. This suggested a positive effect on their sense of control and resiliency via involved, well-developed service-learning activities. At the very least, a new and transformational understanding of the needs of others will help children exposed to trauma focus on something other than their own difficulties, and this alone can be life-changing for some. For these reasons, service-learning programs should stipulate goals that go beyond merely academic achievement and assistance in the community, to include goals inclusive of increased empathy and increased motivation to be involved with others.

Quality of Service Learning

The standards published by the NYLC (n.d.), presented in Box 10.1, provide excellent guidance for structuring high-quality service-learning opportunities. As those standards indicate, the most effective arrangement for service learning is development of a service-learning plan in which service learning is organized in relation to specific academic courses within the curriculum as well as the needs of a community-based partner organization. For example, offering service learning in association with a community for older residents will be different from offering students the opportunity to grow vegetables on campus for distribution to the school cafeteria or the local food bank. The former focus will involve students in direct help of individuals, whereas the latter goals, though quite worthy, do not include excessive face-to-face time helping others.

Box 10.1 Standards for high-quality service learning

- **Meaningful service:** Service learning actively engages participants in meaningful and personally relevant service activities.
- **Reflection:** Service learning incorporates multiple challenging reflection activities that are ongoing and that prompt deep thinking and analysis about oneself and one's relationship to society.
- **Youth voice:** Service learning provides youth with a strong voice in planning, implementing, and evaluating service-learning experiences with guidance from adults.
- **Progress monitoring:** Service learning engages participants in an ongoing process to assess the quality of implementation and progress toward meeting specified goals and uses results for improvement and sustainability.
- **Links to curriculum:** Service learning is intentionally used as an instructional strategy to meet learning goals and/or content standards.
- **Diversity:** Service learning promotes understanding of diversity and mutual respect among all participants.
- **Partnerships:** Service-learning partnerships are collaborative, are mutually beneficial, and address community needs.
- **Duration and intensity:** Service learning has sufficient duration and intensity to address community needs and meet specified outcomes (NYLC, n.d.).

Further, the quality of the community partners providing the placement or setting for the service learning must be considered. A quality partner organization will take the service-learning opportunity seriously and will agree to participate in planning the activity. Further, the partner agency should commit some time and resources to management of the students while they are serving in that setting. Clearly, public school teachers may not be on site during all service-learning activities for all students, so a high level of communication between the service-learning site and the teacher is critical in ensuring quality learning experiences.

Finally, any courses that include service-learning opportunities should have clearly stated learning objectives for students to accomplish, both in class and at the service-learning site. These objectives should address real community needs and involve students in both service activities and structured reflection on the service provided (NYLC, n.d.).

Duration of Service Learning

The duration of the service-learning project—the actual time that students commit to the services they provide to others—will have a great impact on the efficacy of the project both for the students and for those receiving the services (Mabry, 1998). For example, a "service-learning day" once a year can heighten awareness of issues confronted by various community members and thus can be educational for the students, but such an activity is not likely to affect academic outcomes or social skills of the students, and it will certainly not increase their engagement within the community in any profound sense. More time involvement by the students is needed to truly impact academic and social skill outcomes.

In terms of the minimum time needed, Mabry (1998) recommended a commitment of between 15 and 19 hours in direct service. In school terms, this time commitment is roughly an hour a week for approximately half of the school year, which is probably the most useful planning time frame. For example, a half-year commitment to a community partner might involve 25 students for on-site service one hour per week. This semester-long planning idea involves less risk for a school than a yearlong commitment, since once the service learning begins, school personnel may discover that the community partner is not fully committed to the placement or fails to provide supervision as needed. In that case, the school would be free to seek additional or even alternative community partners for the second semester should that become necessary.

Intensity and Goals of Service Learning

The intensity of these service activities must also be considered as a factor affecting efficacy, depending on the desired outcomes for the students. Intensity of any experience involves more than merely the time committed to the experience. Intensity also includes the depth of emotional involvement students have and perhaps even the empathy they develop for others during the service-learning activity. For example, a responsibility to visit with and assist the same older person for an hour each week over the course of a year is much more emotionally intense than a group project based on cleaning a vacant lot near the school to create a local park. In this example, the direct contact with an older person in need is potentially a more emotionally demanding personal experience than yard cleanup. If one goal of the service learning is to increase both social skills and empathy among students, then a more intense experience such as caring for others is more desirable.

With that noted, the lot cleanup option mentioned is much more easily integrated into the school curriculum (e.g., deciding, in courses such as biology or health, which plants to put in the park), and thus, the academic impact among students of this type of service learning might be more easily demonstrated. In this way, the type and intensity of the service-learning experience developed by the school will largely dictate the goals the school faculty might set, as well as the types of positive outcomes that might reasonably be anticipated.

Reflection on the Service-Learning Experience

Virtually all the research on service learning demonstrates that in-depth reflection on the service-learning experience is critical to obtaining the desired outcomes (Billig, 2011; Celio, Durlak, & Dymnicki, 2011; Conway et al., 2009; Durlak, Weissberg, Dymnicki, Taylor, & Schellinger, 2011; Furco & Root, 2010; Sykes et al., 2017). It is during the reflective process that students develop their insight into the issues represented by the various service sites. For example, assisting veterans with disabilities through the local Veterans of Foreign Wars chapter once a week as a service-learning project is likely to develop a different set of insights and understandings than assisting other older persons. Assisting veterans may help students better understand recent history, whereas assisting older individuals will likely develop empathy for older citizens, as well as insight into how society deals with older individuals as a sociological issue. In short, the academic insights developed will largely depend on the community partner options utilized.

However, most of the actual reflection activities are likely to take place not at the community partner location but at the school. Some class time will be utilized for these reflection activities, and the more integrated they are within the course curriculum, the more likely one is to see academic improvements among the students. A variety of activities can be used for such reflection, such as written assignments, regularly scheduled discussions, or even individual and group media presentations (Spring et al., 2008).

Further, learning occurs best within a repetitive cycle of service activity and reflection on the activity, so teachers should not make the mistake of thinking that a single required "reflective paper" at the end of a service-learning semester will suffice. Rather, reflection should be ongoing, beginning with the first visit to the community partner side, so activities such as journaling, individual "service-learning logs," or even a jointly written "service-learning wiki" will result in more and higher-quality reflection experiences than a term paper at the end of the experience. A wiki or class blog would be an ideal teaching tool to make joint socially based reflection an option. Further, each of these activities exposes all student reflection to the other students as well as the teacher, which can be of benefit because students might tend to spend more time on work that will be seen by their peers.

IMPLEMENTATION STEPS FOR SERVICE LEARNING

In considering service learning, proponents state that both the needs and the goals of the schools, as well as the needs of the community, should be considered from the earliest planning discussions onward. Initially, school administrators, teachers, and counselors should consider their schedule, curricular demands, transportation options (students will need some type of transportation to one or more service-learning sites in the community), and the time commitment to the service activities (CNCS, 2007; NYLC, n.d.). Within those possible constraints, schools must also consider which community partner organizations might provide service-learning sites and the needs of those partner organizations. Here are several steps that can help guide educators during the implementation process (Cheek, 2016; Furco, 2011).

Form a Joint Planning Committee

Initially, a planning committee should be formed to develop the service-learning requirement and oversee service-learning activities during the initial year or two of operation. The planning committee for implementation of service learning at the school level should include all teachers who teach courses that might include a service-learning component, such as teachers of biology, history, or health, as well as any other teachers who may wish to participate. English teachers, as one example, may be included if the proposed service-learning activity involves assisting clients in retirement communities who may have impaired eyesight and may wish to have their books or personal correspondence read to them.

Many proponents of service learning emphasize student leadership throughout the process (Cheek, 2016; Furco, 2011), so in the early planning stages, schools might invite students to participate in the planning committee. Of course, another option is to include students after the initial outline of the service-learning project is developed. The purpose of this joint planning committee will be to oversee the entire service-learning effort, not to evaluate specific students' work in service-learning sites (that job will be done by the teachers of the courses associated with the service-learning requirements). Thus, student involvement at the planning committee level will not result in students gleaning information about other students in service-learning locations.

Identification of Potential Community Partners

Agencies within the community are typically used to provide the locations for the service-learning options for students. These may include assisted living communities, nursing homes, food banks, community cooperatives, disaster relief agencies, veterans' homes, animal shelters, the Salvation Army and other faith-based communities, and many other types of nonprofit agencies in which service to the community of one type or another is offered. If faith-based communities or agencies are included in the service-learning options, an effort should be made to include agencies of all faiths so that students of all religions (or none) may have an option for service. Once one or more community partners are identified, those agencies should be invited to have someone sit on the planning committee to ensure completely open communication between the school and all involved community partner organizations.

Statement of Goals, Activities, and Time Commitments

During the first planning session, the committee should develop a set of broad goals for the service-learning requirement, and these may include statements such as the number of students participating; the service time frame (e.g., one hour per week for 15 weeks or something similar); the academic, behavioral, or other outcomes desired from the project; or other goals that research suggests may be attained via service learning (Billig, 2011; Mabry, 1998; Sykes et al., 2017). With children exposed to trauma in mind, we recommend including both academic and social-emotional goals for the service-learning program.

After a list of goals is developed, a statement should be created on the broad types of activities that students may undertake at the host sites as well as a firm time commitment stating how long and how often students will provide service. The community partner organizations will need this information to determine how many of their clients the students can provide service for and when such service might be scheduled each week.

Once the broad description of the service-learning opportunities and time frames is developed, parents should be notified of the service-learning option. In some cases, schools seek permission of the parents prior to offering a service-learning course to the students, but in other cases (e.g., instances in which service learning is a requirement for graduation), schools may simply inform the parents of the child's requirement and the locations where the service-learning work might be completed.

Develop Course-Related Goals, Objectives, and Content Standards

While the planning committee will be primarily responsible for developing the overall plan and goals for service learning as well as identification of the community partner sites for the service, the teachers associated with courses involved in the service-learning effort will take primary responsibility for listing goals, objectives, and content standards for the service learning. Historically, this specificity of standards and course objectives for service learning has been one point of failure in many service-learning programs, simply because no specific objectives were identified for the service learning other than a required number of hours of service.

This is why modern guidelines for effective service learning stipulate development of course-related objectives. Further, the teachers know the curricular content in their respective subject areas and thus should be the primary authority in determining which objectives might be accomplished through the service-learning project and which will require other types of in-class activities.

Develop Formative Progress Monitoring Tools

Associated with the objectives and content standards within the service-learning requirements, each teacher should likewise develop progress monitoring assessments of some type that will help document student progress in the service-learning requirement. Again, mere documentation of hours of service is not sufficient for high-quality service-learning projects, so various types of assessments will be needed. For example, progress monitoring tools may include case studies written by students, structured post-semester interviews with those served, surveys of those at the service site, research papers on social issues associated with the service, or group media presentations. Teachers should use their imagination and the input of the students and community service partners to determine what types of assessments might be appropriate.

In addition to various progress monitoring assignments for the students, observations of the students during service learning should be included. Such observations take time, so these will be limited, but both the teachers using service learning and the community partners may be used to observe students and thus provide guidance not only for the service provided but for how the student views the service responsibilities.

Finally, the standards for effective service learning, as well as virtually all research on efficacy of service learning (Billig, 2011; Celio et al., 2011; Conway et al., 2009; Furco & Root, 2010), strongly emphasize the critical nature of reflective thought throughout the service-learning activities. As for the progress monitoring planning described earlier, appropriate reflective activities to take place on a regular basis throughout the service-learning experience should be developed by the teachers involved. Both individual and group reflective activities should be included, and all types of learning activities can be used to provide high-quality reflection options.

Like almost all kids, students exposed to trauma probably benefit most from the reflective assignments associated with service learning, since reflections on the actual service activities are, in all probability, the point at which the students develop empathy, a sense of their own self-efficacy, and a sense of personal control. This truly is the richness of service learning for kids exposed to trauma. For this reason, self-reports and other reflective activities are great options for these programs.

Set a Site Visit Schedule and Begin Service Learning

At this point, the sites for the service have been identified, parents informed, schedules set, objectives stipulated, and assessments planned and developed. The actual service activities of the students have, at this point, been planned, and thus the service activities should begin. Because these service visits will, of necessity, be tied somewhat to school scheduling, half-year or full-year service visits are typically what schools plan for. However, early in the service, the teachers of the courses associated with service learning will need to hold more in-class discussions and follow up on the service activities in order to ensure that things are beginning in the right way. After the students have made several visits to the service site, the need for in-class monitoring discussions diminishes to some degree.

Evaluation of the Program

After one or two months of service site visits, the overall planning committee will need to meet once again and begin to monitor progress, not of the individual students but of the program as a whole. General data should be collected relative to how often students visited service-learning sites and how often reflective activities were taking place. While individual student issues are primarily the teacher's responsibility, the committee may need to, on occasion, troubleshoot any problems that may have arisen.

At a minimum, the planning committee will need to develop data on the ongoing activities of the program in order to document the successes and failures of the effort. In some extreme circumstances, community partners may need to be reconsidered if the students are not receiving appropriate service-learning time.

PROVEN OUTCOMES OF SERVICE LEARNING

The number of public schools providing service learning continues to increase for one simple reason: Service learning works. Research has consistently shown the efficacy of high-quality service learning in a variety of outcome areas (Billig, 2011; Celio et al., 2011; Drew, 2023; Furco & Root, 2010; NCES, 2023). Positive effects of service learning include increased academic skills, increased self-concept, increased empathy for others, increased social skills, increased civic engagement, and improved behavior in school (Durlak et al., 2011; Youth.gov, n.d.).

Celio and colleagues (2011), as one example, conducted a meta-analytic study of 62 service-learning projects involving nearly 12,000 students. Measurable positive benefits were found in a wide variety of areas including positive attitudes toward self, schooling and learning, civil engagement, social skills, and improved academic performance. Students who experienced involved long-term service-learning opportunities were better behaved than other students, developed social skills more quickly, demonstrated improved academic scores compared to others, and developed more positive beliefs about their own potential success in life. All of these benefits have likewise been shown in numerous other studies (Conway et al., 2009), and these are critical skills for students exposed to trauma.

Other data suggest that service learning may be particularly helpful with specific high-risk populations. For example, service learning has been shown to help prevent dropouts (Bridgeland, Dilulio, & Wulsin, 2008; CNCS, 2007) or to help close the achievement gap between students from underrepresented groups and others (Scales & Roehlkepartain, 2005). Research likewise indicates successful implementation with students from lower-income families. Specifically, when children from disadvantaged circumstances participated in school-based service learning, they were more likely to be engaged and believe in their ability to make a difference in their community (CNCS, 2007). These students from lower-income homes felt more empowered in service learning than in traditional instructional formats, sensing that their contributions in the service venue were important. As stated previously, this "self-efficacy" factor—the ability to have control over one's environment—is critical for students exposed to trauma. Thus, service learning seems to be an excellent intervention for all such students.

SUMMARY

Service learning is an instructional approach that, while different from traditional instruction, holds potential to make instruction meaningful for students exposed to multiple adverse childhood experiences (ACEs). The research clearly documents efficacy of service learning when high standards are used in developing the program, the duration and intensity are sufficient to meet the stated program goals, progress monitoring is ongoing, and students are provided multiple ongoing opportunities to reflect on their experiences. Further, this strategy, unlike most others in education, offers the opportunity to fundamentally change students' perceptions of others in society. In a quality service-learning experience, students not only develop empathy for others, critical for students living with trauma, but may also acquire a sense of their own self-efficacy in making things better for someone else.

Finally, given the need to transform neural connections of students exposed to repeated trauma in order to help them succeed, this strategy seems particularly appropriate for students exposed to multiple ACEs. For these reasons, service learning is one strategy that virtually all schools should implement. The time commitment to developing a high-quality service-learning project will be more than paid for by the time saved not dealing with behavioral problems of kids exposed to trauma, so we do recommend this strategy for virtually all schools.

REFERENCES

Billig, S. H. (2011). Making the most of your time: Implementing the K–12 learning standards for quality practice. *Prevention Researcher*, *18*(1), 8–13.

Bridgeland, J. M., Dilulio, J. J., Jr., & Wulsin, S. C. (2008). *Engaged for success: Service-learning as a tool for high school dropout prevention*. Civic Enterprises.

Celio, C. L., Durlak, J., & Dymnicki, A. (2011). A meta-analysis of the impact of service-learning on students. *Journal of Experiential Education*, *34*(2), 164–181.

Cheek, K. (2016). *Six steps for successful service learning*. Project Learning Tree. Retrieved from https://www.plt.org/educator-tips/6-steps-for-successful-service-learning/

Chemtob, C. M., Novaco, R. W., Hamada, R. S., Gross, D. M., & Smith, G. (1997). Anger regulation deficits in combat-related posttraumatic stress disorder. *Journal of Traumatic Stress*, *10*(1), 17–35.

Conway, J. M., Amel, E. L., & Gerwien, D. P. (2009). Teaching and learning in the social context: A meta-analysis of service learning's effects on academic, personal, social, and citizenship outcomes. *Teaching of Psychology*, *36*, 233–245.

Corporation for National and Community Service. (2007). Leveling the path to participation: Volunteering and civic engagement among youth from disadvantaged circumstances. In *Brief 3 in the Youth Helping America Series*. Corporation for National and Community Service.

Doidge, N. (2007). *The brain that changes itself*. Penguin Books.

Drew, C. (2023, October 26). *18 service learning examples*. Helpful Professor. Retrieved from https://helpfulprofessor.com/service-learning-examples/#google_vignette

Durlak, J. A., Weissberg, R. P., Dymnicki, A. B., Taylor, R. D., & Schellinger, K. B. (2011). The impact of enhancing students' social and emotional learning: A meta-analysis of school-based universal interventions. *Child Development*, *82*, 405–432.

Furco, A. (2011, October). Service-learning: A balanced approach to experiential education. *The International Journal for Global and Development Education Research*, 71–76. Retrieved from http://educacio-cp89.webjoomla.es/wp-content/uploads/03-Furco-1-English.pdf

Furco, A., & Root, S. (2010). Research demonstrates the value of service learning. *Phi Delta Kappan, 91*(5), 16–20.

Knapp, T. D., & Bradley, J. F. (2010). The effectiveness of service-learning: It's not always what you think. *Journal of Experiential Education, 33*(3), 208–224.

Mabry, J. B. (1998). Pedagogical variations in service-learning and student outcomes: How time, contact, and reflection matter. *Michigan Journal of Community Service Learning, 5*, 32–47.

National Center for Education Statistics. (2023). *Service learning and community service in K–12 public schools.* Retrieved from https://nces.ed.gov/surveys/frss/publications/1999043/index.asp?sectionid=5

National Youth Leadership Council. (n.d.). *Service-learning K–12 standards.* Retrieved from https://nylc.org/k-12-standards/

Perry, B. D. (2000). Children exposed to trauma: How childhood trauma influences brain development. *The Journal of the California Alliance for the Mentally Ill, 11*(1), 48–51.

Perry, B. D. (2014). *Helping children exposed to trauma: A brief overview for caregivers.* ChildTrauma Academy. Retrieved from https://www.childtrauma.org/_files/ugd/aa51c7_237459a7e16b4b7e9d2c4837c908eefe.pdf

Scales, P. C., & Roehlkepartain, E. C. (2005). Can service-learning help reduce the achievement gap? New research points toward the potential of service-learning for low-income students. In J. Kielsmeier & M. Neal (Eds.), *Growing to greatness 2005: The state of service-learning in the United States* (pp. 10–22). National Youth Leadership Council.

Spring, K., Grimm, R., & Dietz, N. (2008, November). *Community service and service-learning in America's schools.* Corporation for National and Community Service. Retrieved from https://files.eric.ed.gov/fulltext/ED506728.pdf

Sykes, B. E., Pendley, J., & Deacon, Z. (2017). Transformative learning, tribal membership, and cultural restoration: A case study of an embedded Native American service-learning project at a research university. *Gateways: International Journal of Community Research and Engagement, 10*, 204–228.

Thomsen, J. (2014, January). *State policies on service-learning.* Education Commission of the States. Retrieved from https://www.ecs.org/clearinghouse/01/10/66/11066.pdf

Youth.gov. (n.d.). *Service-learning.* Retrieved from https://youth.gov/youth-topics/civic-engagement-and-volunteering/service-learning

CHAPTER 11

RESTORATIVE JUSTICE

RESTORATIVE JUSTICE IN SCHOOLS

Evolution of Restorative Justice Practices

Restorative justice evolved from practices within the juvenile justice system (Davis, 2014a; Fronius, Persson, Guckenburg, Hurley, & Petrosino, 2016) and is increasingly emphasized in schools as an alternative to in-school and out-of-school suspensions (Johnes, 2023; O'Drobrinak & Kelley, 2021). The original concept of restorative justice involved having perpetrators of bad behavior discuss the behavior with the victims to understand the negative impact of their bad behaviors, as well as resolve any conflict that may have led to the confrontation. The goal was to restore a more appropriate, respectful relationship between perpetrators and victims (Davis, 2014b; O'Brien, 2014; St. George, 2014). This practice has been recommended specifically for students exposed to trauma when these students experience conflict in schools (O'Drobrinak & Kelley, 2021), because it tends to strengthen empathy. Also, unlike many of the classroom-based interventions presented here, this strategic intervention is probably most effective when implemented on a schoolwide basis, making this an important option for schools seeking to become trauma sensitive.

Restorative justice may be defined as practices and activities that restore students' positive relationships with victims and others in the school environment (Johnes, 2023; O'Brien, 2014). The idea behind restorative practices is that, rather than simply removing a student from the classroom (as do more traditional punishments such as in-school or out-of-school suspension), restorative justice practices help misbehaving students understand the injury they cause. Over time, these practices help build healthy relationships and a sense of community among all students in the school, which tends to prevent further conflict (Davis, 2014b; O'Brien, 2014; St. George, 2014). For students exposed to trauma, these procedures will help them reconnect with others in the classroom. Further, restorative justice disciplinary practices are intended to allow students who have violated rules to take responsibility for their behavior while remaining in the school setting. Finally, restorative practices are more likely to help address the issues underlying problem behaviors, rather than just the behavior problems themselves.

Restorative Circles for Conflict Resolution

Courts and schools have tended to implement restorative justice differently. Restorative circles are perhaps the most commonly used restorative justice technique in schools. Sometimes referred to as "talking circles" or "dialog circles," these circle discussions may involve the entire class to improve class climate. However, in most cases, they include only the students involved in a conflict, the teacher, perhaps parents or caregivers, and an administrator in an effort to resolve a conflict. In fact, there is a significant overlap between conflict resolution practices and the restorative justice circle. Both involve having two parties in a dispute discuss the confrontation or conflict, share their experiences, and then generate alternatives that might help resolve the conflict and alleviate future conflicts. Because of these similarities, conflict resolution and restorative justice practices are often described together (Davis, 2014a; O'Drobrinak & Kelley, 2021).

A restorative circle is a wonderful technique for use with children exposed to trauma because the trauma in their background may prevent them from understanding the harm their misbehaviors might due to others. In a restorative circle, it is quite common for students exposed to trauma to learn that what they perceived as a threat was not, in fact, threatening, and this is a huge reason to use this technique. Restorative circles also teach conflict avoidance, conflict resolution, and empathy for others, all of which are essential lessons for children exposed to trauma. The companion website for this book (https://traumahelpnow.com) presents a list of videos on restorative justice practices, and we urge teachers to review one or more of those should they choose to implement this strategy.

An Administrator's Use of Restorative Circles

Victoria Halferty, MSEd, earned degrees from the University of Georgia and the University of Scranton (Pennsylvania). Dr. Bender had the honor to teach Ms. Halferty in her undergraduate work and has followed her career ever since. She has taught students with special needs for 13 years and spent the past 11 years as an administrator in Reading, Pennsylvania, with both disciplinary and instructional leadership responsibilities. She has led the effort in several schools to institute restorative practices and has personally used restorative circles to reduce conflict among students. She is committed to this approach, and her experience is quite informative.

Vignette 11.1 Educator's perspective on restorative circles

After only two days of restorative practices in Bethlehem, Pennsylvania, in 2008, I discovered that what I once recognized as "old-fashioned, just plain talking and listening" is fundamentally effective for managing students with behavioral issues. What a wonderful, though hidden, discovery! The caring, effective listening skills of my family, and in particular of my grandparents—my most admired educators—were linked with my educational experiences by very simple, fundamental guidelines for lifetime learning. Developing genuine conversational skills—reaching toward a common understanding with open listening and thoughtful speaking—is the most valuable factor in rich teaching and effective discipline. To have these conversations with students demonstrating behavioral problems, clearly defined and structured, will build communities supportive of appropriate behavior and learning, a precious goal indeed. After implementing restorative circles within my academic and behavioral practices as an educator, my need for writing referrals to the administration became very limited, as many behavioral problems melted away. My experience as a professional educator and lifelong learner was redefined with regard to my own personal responsibility for truly engaging my students and developing the art of restorative and meaningful conversations.

Restorative practices return us to an old and effective way of encouraging the human spirit toward growth. People who know they are able to speak honestly, freely, and thoughtfully to others within defined parameters are able to quickly build and develop mutual goals. These practices allow teachers to develop as the "lead" learners in the educational environment, and the students are able to develop as mutually dependent on one another for cooperative, cordial, and positive feedback while building knowledge! As this recognition of mutual learning grows, so does the capacity of the entire learning community.

Restorative practices are not only necessary in the 21st century classroom; they are essential in a time when the digital environment leaves the humanistic world in the past. Without intentional conversations toward behavioral improvement and meaningful learning, our professional efforts to foster appropriate behavior and to direct students toward lifelong learning are futile.

STEPS IN A RESTORATIVE CIRCLE INTERVENTION

As with most of these strategies, different schools implement this process in different ways (Davis, 2014b; Johnes, 2023). Some schools use restorative circles with the entire class, whereas others use them as a disciplinary response to a behavioral problem, such as a fight in the classroom or a bullying episode. In that application of the restorative circle, this process serves the same disciplinary function as the practice of suspension, while having the participants in the altercation actually talk to each other in a structured manner. With these differences noted, the eight steps presented as follows seem to be common to most restorative circle interventions (Davis, 2014b; Johnes, 2023; PBS NewsHour, 2014). In many cases, school districts prepare forms that encompass most of these steps.

Report the Behavioral Incident

Most restorative circles in schools are held in response to a single disciplinary occurrence, and that event is typically serious in nature. Fighting, having a weapon in school, or bullying may be instances in which teachers would initiate a restorative circle, and if legal issues are involved, the principal must be notified immediately and may choose to participate. Teachers should document via a short paragraph exactly what they saw or what other students reported about the behavioral problem.

Schedule the Restorative Circle

In most cases, teachers schedule a circle for after school because parents are typically involved, and the school administrative assistant manages the logistics of scheduling. For serious infractions, it is critical to have all involved students and their parents attend, as well as the teacher and an administrator. Depending on training, some schools have the guidance counselor or a school administrator actually facilitate the restorative circle conference. Others who may be involved include special education teachers, school resource officers, and the school psychologist, as appropriate.

Conduct an Initial Narrative Presentation

This step and the steps that follow take place during the restorative circle itself. The meeting facilitator begins the meeting by presenting the initial statement of the problem. This should occur in a nonjudgmental, statement-of-facts manner, because for parents and others who may not yet know exactly what happened, this may be the first time they hear any details about the behavioral incident.

Have Participants State Their Perspectives

Next, the main participants—the students (or in some cases a student and the teacher)—state their description of what happened. These persons will frequently disagree with the initial statement by the facilitator, so the meeting facilitator makes notes on disagreements and points them out as they arise. The facilitator gives each of the students in the conflict the opportunity to state their perception of the events without being interrupted by the other participants. Teachers may also be invited to state their perspectives, particularly if the presenting conflict was between a student and a teacher.

Although parents of students in conflict are not required to verbally participate in any steps, the facilitator might invite their contribution, beginning at this point and continuing in subsequent steps. In some cases, parents may have critical information to share. For example, they may note that their child has been complaining at home of an ongoing problem with the other person in the conflict. If such relevant information is presented, it should be noted also.

Point Out Areas of Agreement/Disagreement

After students and teachers are heard and parents are given an opportunity to speak, the meeting facilitator should point out areas of agreement while mentioning that those agreements may become the initial steps toward restoring a positive relationship. Next, the disagreements in perspective are discussed. The facilitator might ask one or both of the participants if they understand how the other person may have perceived the conflict differently. In some cases, it might be useful to have participants take the other side of the argument or try to explain why the other person involved might have done what they did or said what they said.

For students exposed to trauma, the ability to take the perspective of someone else can be difficult. The skill of perspective taking is often not well developed in home environments that include abusive behavior, so this step often represents a steep learning curve for many kids exposed to trauma. In fact, when restorative circles are used for these students, it is quite possible that this step alone becomes one of the most important elements in the entire process.

Have Students Take Responsibility

Next, the meeting facilitator asks the participants if they would be willing to take responsibility for how the other party interpreted their actions. In some cases, the facilitator might ask students to apologize to the other party. Again, parents can be critical here in helping motivate students to take responsibility for their actions. If punishment is to be used in a particular instance, having students agree to accept the punishment by taking responsibility for their actions is also emphasized.

Discuss Alternatives

Next, the meeting facilitator leads a brief brainstorming session to try to find mutually acceptable interaction options that may reduce or eliminate similar conflicts in the future. Options should be listed on paper or a dry-erase board for future discussion. Then the group discusses each option and chooses one or more to implement.

Sign an Agreement

Finally, the meeting facilitator asks the students in conflict to sign an agreement stating that they will manage any potential conflict in the future using one of the alternatives generated in the previous discussion. The final written agreement thus represents a signed commitment on the part of the students. This emphasis on "signing" may help students understand the seriousness of their commitment, and thus motivate them to live by that agreement. Most restorative circle agreements also stipulate a follow-up meeting or, in some cases, several such meetings.

A RESTORATIVE CIRCLE CASE STUDY

As noted previously, many school districts develop a case study form that delineates the steps of a restorative circle intervention and provides space for the facilitator to write up the various sections of the report. A case study using such a report form is found in Box 11.1. Although each of the steps is not represented by a section on the form, most are. Also, the final part of this report shows that the planned follow-up to the restorative circle meeting is typically held about 10 days to two weeks after the restorative circle. In this example, the notes show that both of the students have honored their commitments and that no subsequent fights have taken place after the restorative circle. At this point, the principal considers the problem resolved.

Box 11.1 Restorative justice circle report form

Students Involved: *Tracy Sparks, Timothy Attwood*   **Date of the Problem:** *9/2/23*

Class or Location: *Mr. Trotter's Science Class (Second Period)*

Date of Restorative Circle: *9/5/23*   **Conflict:** *Physical Fighting in Class*

School Persons Involved:
Because a fight was involved, Ms. Waller, the assistant principal, requested that Mr. Lerma, the school resource officer, attend the meeting. Mr. Trotter was also present.

Report of Behavioral Incident—Teacher's Perspective:
On September 2, 2019, at 10:30 a.m., I told the class to get out their science books. A moment later, I looked up, and Timothy was standing over Tracy's desk with his science book in the air, and then Timothy brought the book down on Tracy's head. I rushed over there, but by the time I got there Thomas Gibson was holding Timothy, backing him away, and Tracy was on the floor with his forehead bleeding. I told Timothy to sit down in an empty desk across the classroom and sent another student to get the principal and the school nurse. We wiped Tracy's head with a paper towel.

Students' Perspectives:
Timothy: He was looking at me funny, and I heard him call me an a**hole.
Tracy: Timothy calls me names every day—dickhead, bitch, a**hole, slimeball—and he won't stop. He called me a slimeball that day, so I called him an a**hole. Then he grabbed a book and hit me.

Areas of Agreement/Disagreement:
Both students state that they have never been friends and have no desire to become friends. They "move in different circles." Also, they both see the dangers of spreading rumors around school and using inappropriate names for each other. Each was asked how it felt to be called names in front of his friends, and each understood that it hurt other people when they were called names.

Options for Reducing Conflict: *The students decided that it is best to eliminate this problem and that they could do the following:*

- ▸ *Just ignore each other*
- ▸ *Always sit apart from each other in the two classes they have in common*
- ▸ *Avoid each other on school campus (lunchroom, commons, library, etc.)*
- ▸ *Never call each other names or interact with each other*
- ▸ *Not talk about each other, even when the other one is not around*

(Continued)

(Continued)

Further, both students agreed that fighting was against the rules, and some punishment was appropriate. Both agreed to help our janitor pick up trash on the school yard for three recess periods, during the next week. Ms. Waller will monitor that work, and be informed by the janitor if the students do not cooperate in that work.

Commitment:

By our signatures below, we agree to behave in the manner we've chosen, and do the things listed above as punishment for fighting. We also agree to eliminate any conflict between us. If either of us breaks this agreement, we understand that the harshest punishment will go to the first one of us to break these new rules. Also, we understand that hitting is against the law, and that the police may become involved if either of us is hit by the other one again.

Timothy Attwood	*Tracy Sparks*
Ms. Laura Waller, Asst. Prin.	*9/5/23*
Facilitator's Signature	Date

Planned Follow-Up:

► *While parents were invited to this meeting, neither came, but both asked to be kept informed, so Ms. Waller will share this report with the parents of each student.*
► *Ms. Waller and Mr. Trotter will meet with these two students after school on 9/21/23 as a follow-up, and again after a further six weeks. At each meeting, we will consider any problems between these students, and reemphasize the commitments made above.*

First Follow-Up Meeting:

On the afternoon of September 21, Mr. Trotter and Ms. Waller met with these students. Parents were invited to attend, and Tracy's mom did come to this meeting. Ms. Waller indicated that she had not heard of any interactions between these students, nor has Mr. Trotter or any other teacher reported any. Both students said they had stayed away from each other, and neither reported any name-calling. Mr. Trotter said that he hoped that the two young men might become friends one day, but that it was up to them. Both students reaffirmed their commitment to follow the rules above to avoid any conflict. Ms. Waller indicated that unless further problems between these boys are seen, the second follow-up meeting may be canceled.

RESEARCH ON RESTORATIVE CIRCLES

There is a growing research base for restorative justice in schools (Fronius et al., 2016; Johnes, 2023; McCold, 2008; Petrosino, Guckenburg, & Fronius, 2012). For example, Fronius and his colleagues (2016) reviewed available research on restorative justice in schools and demonstrated that a well-implemented restorative justice program will reduce punitive disciplinary actions and problem behaviors in the schools overall. Several studies in different middle and high schools around the United States documented a more than 80% drop in out-of-school suspension when restorative circles were implemented (Armour, 2013; Davis, 2014a). Clearly this provides a good disciplinary option for principals to use instead of suspension.

Further, the longer a student is exposed to restorative justice practices like the restorative circle, the more positive the impact. McCold (2008) reported that recidivism rates changed based on exposure to restorative justice practices, with youth who completed the restorative justice program showing more reduction in behavioral infractions compared to others. Further analysis suggested that participants who completed the restorative justice process demonstrated positive increases in self-esteem and prosocial attitudes.

Other evidence documents the benefits of restorative justice practices in areas other than exclusion from school (Jain, Bassey, Brown, & Kalra, 2014; McMorris, Beckman, Shea, Baumgartner, & Eggert, 2013). McMorris and colleagues (2013) showed that a restorative circle program in Minnesota resulted in reduced self-reported incidents of physical fighting and skipping school among conference participants. Jain and his coworkers (2014) showed reductions of 24% in chronic absenteeism among schools using restorative justice practices.

Finally, Johnes (2023) points to many other benefits of restorative justice practices, including promoting social-emotional learning, teaching conflict resolution skills, and increasing empathy, as well as helping students develop problem-solving skills. As these benefits indicate, this intervention directly addresses many of the issues teachers and counselors confront when serving students exposed to trauma, suggesting that restorative circles are one practice that almost all schools should consider in order to prepare for students exposed to trauma.

SUMMARY

Restorative justice practices are one of several specific innovations promoted by the proponents of trauma-informed schools for two reasons (Johnes, 2023; O'Drobrinak & Kelley, 2021). First, these practices work to reduce disciplinary problems, and second, restorative practices have many benefits that, like other strategies presented in this book, target the specific issues of students exposed to frequent childhood trauma. Cumulatively, these data document the benefits of restorative justice in a variety of ways that are of paramount importance to deeply injured kids, such as reduced fighting, increased empathy, and increased respect among students. Other results show improved self-concept—one component of improving mental health—as well as improvements in social attitudes.

Given these research-documented benefits of restorative justice practices, coupled with the documented numbers of kids exposed to trauma in today's schools, it is reasonable to anticipate that virtually all schools should undertake implementation of restorative justice circles. In fact, failure to implement this set of practices may lead to failure in managing many kids exposed to trauma, as well as other students with behavioral difficulties. Simply put, educators can no longer avoid responsibility for undertaking restorative justice practices, which, like many strategies in this book, have been shown to work for children exposed to trauma.

REFERENCES

Armour, M. (Ed.). (2013). *White middle school restorative discipline evaluation: Implementation and impact, 2012/2013 sixth grade*. Austin: University of Texas.

Davis, F. E. (2014a). Discipline with dignity: Oakland classrooms try healing instead of punishment. *Reclaiming Children and Youth, 23*(1), 38–41.

Davis, F. E. (2014b, September 26). 8 tips for schools interested in restorative justice. *Edutopia*. Retrieved from http://www.edutopia.org/blog/restorative-justice-tips-for-schools-fania-davis

Fronius, T., Guckenburg, S., Hurley, N., & Petrosino, A. (2016). Restorative justice in U.S. schools: A research review. *WestEd*. Retrieved from https://www.wested.org/wp-content/uploads/2016/11/1456766824resourcerestorativejusticeresearchreview-3.pdf

Jain, S., Bassey, H., Brown, M., & Kalra, P. (2014). *Restorative justice implementation and impacts in Oakland schools* (prepared for the Office of Civil Rights, U.S. Department of Education). Oakland Unified School District, Data in Action.

Johnes, S. (2023). Why every school needs a restorative justice approach: 3 examples, and 7 steps guide. *Science and Literacy*. Retrieved from https://scienceandliteracy.org/restorative-justice-in-schools/#google_vignette

McCold, P. (2008). Evaluation of a restorative milieu: Restorative practices in context. *Sociology of Crime, Law and Deviance, 11*, 99–137.

McMorris, B. J., Beckman, K. J., Shea, G., Baumgartner, J., & Eggert, R. C. (2013). *Applying restorative justice practices to Minneapolis Public Schools students recommended for possible expulsion*. University of Minnesota.

O'Brien, A. (2014, May 20). Inequities in student discipline: What to do about them. *Edutopia*. Retrieved from http://www.edutopia.org/blog/inequities-student-discipline-what-to-do-anne-obrien?utm_source=twitter&utm_medium=post&utm_campaign=blog-inequities-discipline

O'Drobrinak, B., & Kelley, B. (2021). *Teaching, learning, + trauma: Responsive practices for holding steady in turbulent times*. Corwin.

PBS NewsHour. (2014, February 20). To curb conflict, a Colorado high school replaces punishment with conversation. Retrieved from https://www.pbs.org/newshour/show/colorado-high-school-replaces-punishment-talking-circles

Petrosino, A., Guckenburg, S., & Fronius, T. (2012). "Policing schools" strategies: A review of the evaluation evidence. *Journal of MultiDisciplinary Evaluation, 8*(17), 80–101. doi:10.56645/jmde.v8i17.337

St George, D. (2014, June 3). Schools get road map for improving discipline practices. *The Washington Post*. Retrieved from https://www.washingtonpost.com/local/education/schools-get-road-map-for-improving-discipline-practices/2014/06/02/da13257c-e8f2-11e3-8f90-73e071f3d637_story.html

EPILOGUE

BRINGING THIS ALL TOGETHER

At this point, it would not be an overstatement to say that teaching students exposed to multiple adverse childhood experiences (ACEs) may be the most challenging teaching any teacher will undertake. Further, even the most highly trained and qualified, veteran teachers will need to have these insights and strategies in order to deal with children exposed to trauma. Also, we sincerely hope that teacher preparation programs across the nation and around the world will consider these needs in preparing teachers for today's classrooms.

As pointed out throughout this book, the brains of these children are "wired" differently, and many hours of successful, enjoyable work and learning experiences are necessary to help reprogram those brains toward more positive moods, behaviors, and modes of thought. As stated in various chapters, trauma-informed schools must accomplish certain things if they are to be optimal environments for helping these children find success:

1. Preparing teachers to understand the warning signs for various types of childhood trauma

2. Ensuring that teachers are informed about the impact of childhood trauma on behavior

3. Helping teachers teach kids about traumatized brains, with great care and sensitivity

4. Assisting teachers to set up their classrooms with students exposed to ACEs in mind

5. Ensuring that teachers teach challenged kids that they can control their moods and emotions

6. Implementing schoolwide practices to foster success

7. Requiring teachers to implement specific intervention strategies proven to work with children exposed to trauma (These will require individual data collection to show efficacy to the child, other professionals, and parents or caregivers of the child.)

The various teaching tactics and specific instructional strategies covered in this book and on the companion website can help school faculty and professional counselors accomplish these tasks. While time is always a concern for practicing professionals, today's classrooms include a number of children who have been exposed to multiple ACEs and many children who were in school during the COVID-19 pandemic. Those students may have experienced the social isolation of that period as some level of mild trauma as a result of online, at-home schooling. Such social isolation has been shown to impact some children more than others in a negative fashion, so the need for becoming a trauma-informed school is, today, greater than ever.

Certainly, all teachers in trauma-informed schools should be instructed in the information on trauma included in Chapter 1 and the information on brain development as impacted by trauma in Chapter 2. Further, all teachers should be implementing a variety of the teaching ideas discussed in Chapters 2, 3, and 4. Many of those tactics are very appropriate in counseling sessions as well as in classrooms.

We believe that some strategies discussed herein are best implemented on a schoolwide level, including the teaching strategies covered in Chapters 9 ("Mentoring Students Exposed to Trauma"), 10 ("Service Learning"), and 11 ("Restorative Justice"). While no school should undertake all these strategies, we believe that trauma-informed schools should be undertaking at least one of these efforts.

Next, parents and caregivers should be prepared to undertake the various teaching strategies covered in other chapters. For example, use of an emotional support animal (Chapter 8) may be implemented by a caring parent or caregiver in the home environment. Likewise, teaching strategies such as mindfulness (Chapter 6) or journaling (Chapter 7) may be implemented in the home. Should parents and/or caregivers undertake these strategies, we certainly recommend informing the teacher and school counselor, as the continuation of these strategies at home may help increase their positive impact. For example, children who engage in journaling at home may wish to share particular journal entries with their teachers on occasion.

Finally, the need for keeping data on specific strategy interventions cannot be overstated. Numerous case studies have been presented in various chapters, and those examples each offer simple data collection guidelines, along with charts to display the success of specific interventions. When an intervention is successful, such data charts speak volumes to children exposed to multiple ACEs as evidence that they can, indeed, manage their moods, emotions, or behaviors. With control being a major concern for children exposed to multiple traumas, showing them the power of such a change in behavior is clearly impactful. It is a small time commitment for teachers, and yet, even the types of simple data charts presented herein can literally change a child's life.

As educators ourselves, we can assure all teachers and counselors that this is the type of professional you will wish to be. Many of you, if not most of you, are at this high professional level already. However, if you are not yet implementing direct targeted interventions and measuring individual children's performance in this fashion, you should begin that practice immediately. In this fashion, and only in this fashion, we all can become more effective change agents in the lives of children exposed to multiple traumas. This is how we find, reach, and teach these students—students who, because of trauma, have not previously been given a real opportunity to succeed. This is the type of teacher we all wish to be.

With that in mind, the authors of this text wish to conclude with an invitation. We invite your school faculty to contact us to join you in this work. We will provide a free 30- to 45-minute dialog, via digital meeting technology, to each school faculty who chooses as a group to undertake this work together. As stated on our companion website, with the purchase of 50 books for use in a schoolwide in-service, we will schedule an online meeting with the schoolwide faculty. This is described at length on the companion website (https://traumahelpnow.com). Should your school not include that many faculty members, we invite you to combine with another school in your district, and we will jointly schedule one 30- to 45-minute online meeting. These online meetings may be a presentation by one of the authors or a simple question-and-answer session. We do this to show our commitment to this important work, and to show our thanks for undertaking this challenge. We look forward to working with you very soon.

INDEX

A Sage Company

Helping educators make the greatest impact

CORWIN HAS ONE MISSION: to enhance education through intentional professional learning.

We build long-term relationships with our authors, educators, clients, and associations who partner with us to develop and continuously improve the best evidence-based practices that establish and support lifelong learning.